NIGEL MANSELL
WORLD CHAMPION

THE STORY OF ONE MAN'S ASCENT TO THE
PINNACLE OF GRAND PRIX STARDOM

BY ALAN HENRY
PHOTOGRAPHS BY PAUL-HENRI CAHIER
HAZLETON PUBLISHING

PUBLISHER
Richard Poulter
EXECUTIVE PUBLISHER
Elizabeth Le Breton
PRODUCTION MANAGER
George Greenfield
ART EDITOR
Tony Baldwin

This first edition published in 1992 by
Hazleton Publishing, 3 Richmond Hill,
Richmond, Surrey TW10 6RE.

ISBN: 1-874557-00-4

Printed in England by Ebenezer Baylis
and Son, Worcester.
Colour reproduction by Adroit Photo
Litho Ltd, Birmingham.

Distributors
UNITED KINGDOM
Bookpoint Limited
39 Milton Park
Abingdon
Oxfordshire OX14 4TD
NORTH AMERICA
Motorbooks International
PO Box 2
729 Prospect Avenue
Osceola
Wisconsin
54020, USA

PICTURE CREDITS
Front cover photograph:
Peter Nygaard
Back cover photograph:
Paul-Henri Cahier
Most of the photographs appearing in
this book were contributed by
Paul-Henri Cahier.
The remainder were supplied by: **Diana
Burnett** pages 20 (inset), 28, 50, 61 and
95; **Steve Domenjoz** pages 8/9, 54/55
(left) and 62/63 (inset); **Lukas Gorys**
page 34 (left); **International Press
Agency** page 16 (inset); **Charles Knight**
page 13 (right); **LAT** pages 62/63 (main
picture) and 69 (inset); **Peter Nygaard**
pages 80/81; **David Phipps** page 27
(inset); **Duncan Raban** pages 18/19
(top); **Keith Randall** pages 12/13; **Nigel
Snowdon** pages 12 (left), 14/15, 16
(bottom), 27 (bottom left), 30/31 (bottom), 34/35, 38/39 (top) and 39
(inset); **John Townsend** pages 40/41
(top) and 50/51; **Vandystadt** pages
56/57 (right); **Zooom Photographic**
pages 86/87, 88/89 and 90/91.

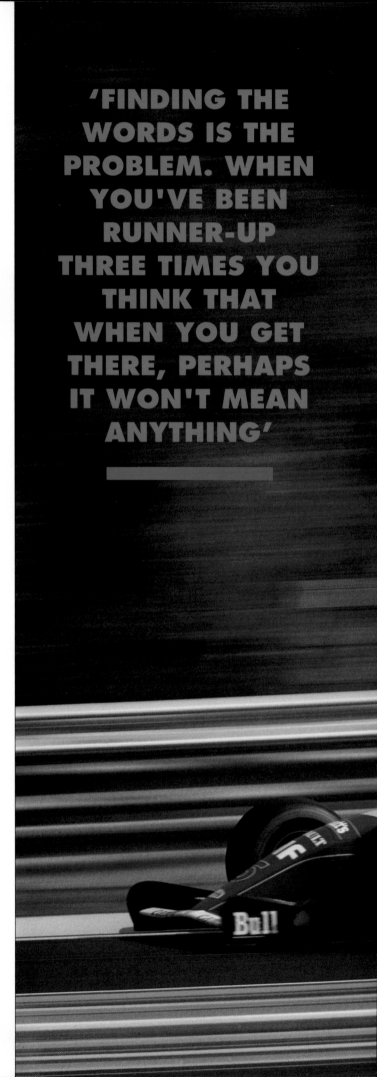

'FINDING THE WORDS IS THE PROBLEM. WHEN YOU'VE BEEN RUNNER-UP THREE TIMES YOU THINK THAT WHEN YOU GET THERE, PERHAPS IT WON'T MEAN ANYTHING'

CONTENTS

MANSELL'S CROWNING ACHIEVEMENT

WHEN NIGEL MANSELL CROSSED THE LINE TO FINISH SECOND IN THE HUNGARIAN GRAND PRIX ON SUNDAY, 16 AUGUST 1992, HE NOT ONLY CLINCHED THE DRIVERS' WORLD CHAMPIONSHIP, BUT ACHIEVED THE REALISATION OF AN AMBITION WHICH HAD BEEN DRIVING HIM RELENTLESSLY ONWARDS, THROUGH GOOD TIMES AND BAD, FOR MORE THAN A DECADE OF GRAND PRIX RACING.

HIS SUCCESS IN THE SPORT'S MOST INTENSELY COMPETITIVE SENIOR CATEGORY HAD NOT BEEN UNRESERVEDLY ANTICIPATED BY EVERYBODY IN THE BUSINESS. IN FACT, THERE WERE MANY WHO BELIEVED MANSELL TO BE LITTLE MORE THAN A YEOMAN RACER: A GOOD, SOLID PERFORMER WHO COULD BE RELIED UPON TO PRODUCE STEADY TOP SIX FINISHES. BUT THE CRITICS AND CYNICS WERE TO BE PROVED WRONG. MANSELL SEIZED EVERY OPPORTUNITY THAT PRESENTED ITSELF WITH A ZEAL AND COMMITMENT THAT WOULD YIELD NO FEWER THAN 29 GRAND PRIX VICTORIES BY THE TIME HE CLINCHED HIS LONG-AWAITED WORLD CHAMPIONSHIP.

MANSELL **SIX**

'THERE IS NO QUESTION THAT WINNING THE WORLD CHAMPIONSHIP IS ONE OF THE GREATEST THINGS IN ANYONE'S LIFE'

STRIVING FOR SUCCESS

MANSELL TOOK LONGER THAN ANY OTHER DRIVER IN HISTORY TO FINALLY CLINCH THE TITLE, BUT IT WAS WORTH THE SLOG

Determined, stubborn, committed, singleminded. ... These are all adjectives which have been applied to Nigel Ernest Mansell throughout his relentless climb towards the glittering pinnacle of his professional motor racing career. Add his immense physical strength, a remarkable affinity with his ever-growing legion of fans and a well-developed sense of theatre and you have the essence of the man who was once firmly cast in a minority when it came to his belief that he would win the World Championship.

To the British public, from whose ranks spring the army of disciples who urge him on from the spectator enclosures, Nigel Mansell's character makes his success all the easier to identify with. In their minds he is one of them, the average man in the street who has made it to the big time, scaling the bastions of

SCENES OF PATRIOTIC EXUBERANCE IN THE WAKE OF MANSELL'S MOMENTOUS 1992 BRITISH GRAND PRIX VICTORY PRODUCED THE REMARKABLE SIGHT OF THE TRACK BEING INVADED BY OVER-ZEALOUS ENTHUSIASTS

MANSELL NINE

**MANSELL WITH
HIS HANDS FULL:
THE DOTING
FAMILY MAN
DURING HIS TIME
AT FERRARI**

sporting success very much against the odds.

Yet the fact that Mansell may seem like the guy they would chat to in the pub conceals quite extraordinary reserves of iron self-belief and British bulldog motivation which have driven him on to the rarefied heights of international Grand Prix stardom.

Meeting him for the first time, one is struck by the strength of his handshake. An experienced motoring journalist once remarked, when he first met Nigel, 'The only other racing driver I've ever met with a handshake like that was James Hunt.' James, of course, was Mansell's immediate predecessor in the role of a British World Champion, winning the title in 1976, sixteen years before Mansell's triumph at the wheel of a Williams-Renault.

To this day, Mansell's Midlands accent has not deserted him. Despite spells living in Portugal and Florida, he is English to the very core of his soul – and patriotically proud of it. For many years after climbing onto the lower rungs of the Formula 1 ladder he lived in the Isle of Man where he still has a bespoke mansion, 'Ballaman', perched on a windswept headland near Port Erin.

He qualified as a member of motor racing's multi-million dollar jet set long ago and is now reputed to be Britain's highest paid sportsman, attracting an annual income thought to be in the region of six million pounds. Yet, in a world where social sharks shadow the superstars, he is a contented family man, very much the home dweller who values his privacy.

Married to his wife Rosanne since 1976, he is a devoted father to Chloe, Leo and Greg. When Rosanne was expecting Greg, Nigel's concern that her pregnancy might run into unexpected trouble was both touching and unconcealed. The challenge of lapping Detroit in his Williams-Honda seemed of secondary importance to him at the time. In that respect, he is a man who has a fine perspective on the priorities of his family life.

Born in Upton-on-Severn on 9 August 1953, Nigel Mansell's initial contact with motor sport was through karting, that bedrock on

'WHEN ROSANNE
WAS EXPECTING
GREG, NIGEL'S
CONCERN...WAS
BOTH TOUCHING
AND UNCON-
CEALED'

CLEAN SHAVEN MANSELL, '88 STYLE (ABOVE), OVER A DECADE AFTER HIS APPRENTICESHIP IN THE ROUGH AND TUMBLE OF FORMULA FORD (RIGHT)

which the careers of so many great stars have been founded. Nigel's self-belief has underpinned his career from the start. What made him different was his sheer persistence and capacity for self-sacrifice as he battled through the ranks of minor league single-seater racing in Formula Ford and Formula 3.

Rosanne has always given him overwhelming support. When, in latter years, one would hear him talking about what 'we' might or might not do in the future, he would be referring to his wife. Nigel never made a single key decision affecting his career without first talking it over with Rosanne. From the nadir of disappointment in F3, through the halcyon days of his Formula 1 ascendancy and on to the crowning glory of his World Champion-

'ROSANNE HAS PROVIDED A SYMPATHETIC SHOULDER FOR NIGEL, LITERALLY AND FIGURATIVELY, THROUGHOUT HIS CAREER'

ship, Rosanne's opinion would always be as important as his own. They are a partnership in the deepest sense of the word.

Before he even graduated to F3, he had been tipped as a potential World Champion. The man who made this prediction was John Thornburn, team manager for Alan McKechnie, the Gloucestershire wine grower who fielded racing cars for sheer pleasure. Thornburn had earlier given a leg-up to the career of Keke Rosberg, another future F1 contender whose immediate promise was not instantly recognised by the touchline pundits.

'I reckon this lad has the best potential since Jim Clark,' said Thornburn

'I WAS IMPRESSED BY THE WAY HE SEEMED T

after Mansell's first few races in the team's Crossle 25F Formula Ford car. It was a strikingly prescient observation and a view shared by two more of his early supporters, journalist Peter Windsor and his fellow-Australian Peter Collins who became assistant Lotus F1 team manager at the start of 1979.

At the 1978 International Trophy, Mansell started his hired March 783 from pole position. Moreover, the way in which the young Englishman hurled his machine through the Woodcote chicane at Silverstone was not going to be lost on the two Peters.

'I was impressed by the way he seemed to be in total control of the whole situation,' remembers Collins. 'He was in pole position, yet he didn't look in the slightest bit flustered or over-awed by it. He seemed completely confident.'

Windsor and Collins quickly became convinced of Mansell's talent and, together, they persuaded Lotus boss Colin Chapman to take an interest. Chapman decided to size up the lad from Birmingham to see if he'd got what it took for F1.

Mansell would grasp his chance with Lotus and fashion it into the launching pad for his Grand Prix aspirations. His first big break came in 1979 when he was invited to join Team Lotus for an F1 test session at Paul Ricard. The trouble was, at the time he received this summons he was languishing in hospital suffering from cracked vertebrae sustained in a Formula 3 collision with Andrea de Cesaris's Ralt at Oulton Park.

This was the second time in his career that serious injuries had thwarted his progress. At Brands Hatch in 1977 he'd sustained broken bones in his neck after a huge Formula Ford shunt and doctors predicted he would

TESTING THE CONTROVERSIAL 'TWIN CHASSIS' LOTUS 88 AT SILVERSTONE IN 1981. BEHIND THE REAR WING, LOTUS BOSS COLIN CHAPMAN WEARS A WORRIED EXPRESSION

be in hospital for months. In fact, he was out within a fortnight and racing again inside six weeks. So when that invitation came to the Paul Ricard test, Nigel accepted with alacrity. Swallowing pain killers like chocolate drops, he made the trip and never allowed anybody to know about his problem.

The Lotus founder was impressed with this new lad's blend of tenacity and irreverence. He was signed on a test contract paying a very modest annual fee of £2500. For both partners, it seemed like an excellent deal.

Chapman quickly grew to admire the young Englishman. By the summer of 1980 he promised Nigel that he would have at least one Grand Prix outing that season in a third Lotus. Mansell's big chance came at the Österreichring where he manhandled the team's third Lotus 81 into last place on the grid.

Just prior to the start, the Lotus sprang a fuel leak into the cockpit, but Mansell gritted his teeth and didn't complain. He raced doggedly at the tail of the field until his machine's Cosworth V8 engine wilted under the strain. He retired, soaked in fuel and with his hamstrings so shrunken by their five-star dousing that Rosanne had to drive him home from London Airport on his return. 'Colin clearly appreciated that here was a man with guts and determination. In fact, he may have seen something of himself in Mansell,' says Peter Collins. Nigel was to have two more Grand Prix outings that season.

At the end of the 1980 season, Chapman's number one driver, Mario Andretti, decided on a switch to Alfa Romeo for what would be his final season in F1. That left the Lotus boss looking for a new man to partner the young Italian, Elio de Angelis. Rightly, under the circumstances, he looked no further

than Nigel.

This was the height of the ground-effect era in F1 engineering technology and Chapman was developing his unique 'twin chassis' Lotus 86 concept, designed to maximise the car's aerodynamic stability while at the same time insulating the driver from the rock-hard suspension which had become such a dreaded factor of this high downforce era. But the concept fell foul of the sport's rule-makers and was promptly banned.

There was little more to come in terms of hard results that season – until the last race of the year which yielded a hard-won fourth place in the inaugural Caesar's Palace GP at Las Vegas. Mansell was 14th in the final World Championship standings with eight points to his credit. Even so, he was brimful of confidence as he looked forward to his second full season with Lotus.

However, 1982's cars still had rock-hard suspension so the drivers continued to be pounded beyond belief. Mansell now inwardly gave thanks that he had put so much effort into weight training and other exhaustive physical preparations in a gymnasium which he had fitted out in his Hall Green, Birmingham, home prior to the start of his serious F1 career.

In the Monaco Grand Prix, the Lotus 91s of Mansell and Elio de Angelis finished fourth and fifth – but had Riccardo Patrese's Brabham BT49D not been successfully push-started after a half-spin on the last lap at the Loews hairpin, victory would have gone to Nigel.

His biggest on-track disappointment that year came in Montreal where his Lotus rode over the left-rear wheel of Bruno Giacomelli's Alfa Romeo as the Italian driver slowed suddenly in preparation for peeling off into the pit lane. Nigel sprained his left forearm.

He missed the Dutch and French Grands Prix, but pulled out all the stops to try and satisfy his fans in the British Grand Prix at

WITH CAST ON LEFT ARM FOLLOWING '82 CANADIAN SHUNT (ABOVE); POLE MAN FOR THE FIRST TIME (RIGHT), DALLAS '84

Nigel Mansell

WITH TEAM-
MATE ELIO DE
ANGELIS
(BOTTOM LEFT),
AND AT MONZA
'82 WITH
LOTUS 91
(BELOW)

Brands Hatch. He qualified and ran near the back of the pack before calling it a day, the bumps and ripples of the Kent circuit being just too much for him to bear.

At the Austrian Grand Prix Nigel had to watch as team-mate Elio de Angelis held off Keke Rosberg's Williams FW08 by less than a wheel to score Lotus's first World Championship win in four years. In the remaining three races that year there were no more points destined to come Mansell's way, a collision with Mauro Baldi's Arrows writing him out of the World Championship finale at Las Vegas .

Worse, by far, was to come. In the early hours of 16 December 1982 Colin Chapman suffered a massive heart attack at his home, East Carleton Manor, a few miles from Team Lotus's Norfolk headquarters at Ketteringham Hall. His death robbed the motor racing scene of one of its greatest and most imaginative engineers. For Nigel Mansell, it was a body blow.

Mansell's cheeky over-familiarity and enormous self-confidence had struck a chord with the Lotus boss. When Mansell finished third at Zolder in 1981, Chapman doubled his retainer. And he doubled it again when he finished fourth at Monaco the following year.

Going into the 1983 season, without Chapman's support, Nigel had to struggle with a Cosworth-engined type 92 for the first few races of the season, while de Angelis used

the first Lotus-Renault turbocar. Yet, ironically, it was Nigel's efforts which saved Team Lotus's bacon with John Player, its long-time sponsors, who were wondering whether or not to continue in 1984.

When the type 93T proved to be a hideously uncompetitive mistake, newly recruited technical director Gérard Ducarouge cobbled together a couple of specials – dubbed 94T – using old type 92 monocoques found in the stores, in time for the British Grand Prix at Silverstone. De Angelis retired early, but Nigel stormed through to take a terrific fourth place. It tipped the scales, and JPS stayed in for 1984. But it had been a close-run thing and Nigel fully deserves recognition for his role in salvaging the deal.

The 1984 season would be Mansell's last with Lotus and it saw him come closer to winning a Grand Prix than ever before. The top place on the rostrum slipped through his fingers at Monaco where, having qualified alongside Alain Prost's McLaren-TAG on the front row of the grid, he took the lead from the Frenchman on lap 11. Over the next five laps, and in monsoon conditions that would eventually see the race flagged to a halt just beyond half-distance, he pulled out more than ten seconds over the Frenchman.

Leading a Grand Prix for the first time – but certainly not for the last – Nigel pushed too hard. He got slightly off-beam on a rain-slicked white line on the climb to Casino Square and clobbered the guard rail. Gathering it all up, he staggered as far as Mirabeau before grinding to a halt. Abandoning his crumpled machine, he sat on the armco, head in hands, as he tried to come to terms with this cruel disappointment.

Yet there was an offer on the table from Frank Williams which was to save Nigel's career. As Mansell would later acknowledge, 'Frank picked me up when I was nothing.' Over the years that followed, the Englishman repaid that faith to spectacular effect.

The move to Williams gave Nigel access to Honda's powerful V6 turbo engines and serious success finally came his way in 1985. Just as his critics were confirming their view that he would never become a winner in F1, he

ECSTASY AND AGONY: HEAD IN HANDS (RIGHT) AFTER CRASHING WHEN LEADING AT A SOAKING MONACO, '84

brought the normally conservative English crowds to their feet in passionate delight with a superb victory in the Grand Prix of Europe at Brands Hatch. It had been eight years since James Hunt's final F1 victory. Britain had another Grand Prix winner at long last!

A few weeks later he followed that success up with a superb victory in South Africa. Williams had given him the key to the winner's rostrum – and Nigel had unlocked it with alacrity! He was up and running as a Grand Prix winner.

Into 1986, armed with the superb new Williams-Honda FW11, he romped away with the Belgian, Canadian, French and Portuguese races as well as scoring his first

JOY DAY AT LAST. VICTORY FINALLY ARRIVED IN THE 1985 EUROPEAN GRAND PRIX FOR WILLIAMS (LEFT). THE LAD HIMSELF CELEBRATES ON THE ROSTRUM (RIGHT)

memorable triumph in the British Grand Prix. That red letter day came at Brands Hatch where, in a race which was initially red-flagged to a halt following a multiple pile-up at Paddock Bend, Nigel stormed to a brilliant victory over team-mate Nelson Piquet's sister car. What made Mansell's success all the more praiseworthy was the fact that he'd had to switch to the spare car for the restart, his race machine having broken a driveshaft accelerating away from the line at the first start.

It was a success which brought a smile to the face of team chief Frank Williams, now confined to a wheelchair following a road accident in France returning from the final pre-season test session at Paul Ricard. Battling to overcome his disability, Williams missed most races that season – but the achievements of his team would be a key motivating factor behind Frank's recovery.

Mansell's superb run of sustained success in the excellent Williams-Honda was destined to carry him to the very verge of the 1986 World Championship. Storming along in third place during the Australian Grand Prix at Adelaide, Nigel was just building up to 195 mph in the slipstream of Philippe Alliot's Ligier as he moved in to lap the French car.

Suddenly the Williams's left-rear tyre exploded. Alliot ducked out of the way as debris began flying, while the Williams sat down on its tyreless rear corner and

SECOND VICTORY CAME AT KYALAMI, '85 (ABOVE) AND NIGEL (RIGHT) FINISHED HIS FIRST SEASON WITH WILLIAMS AS A PROVEN WINNER

MANSELL
CONFERS WITH
FRANK
WILLIAMS. 'HE
PICKED ME UP
WHEN I WAS
NOTHING' CON-
CEDES NIGEL

zigzagged wildly from side to side. Nigel fought valiantly to keep the car off the unyielding concrete barriers and its crazy progress finally petered out at the end of a conveniently situated escape road. The title had slipped from his grasp...

Brushing aside this disappointment, he would be back on the winning trail for Williams-Honda again in 1987, swelling his victory total to 13 wins before a practice accident in the Japanese Grand Prix saw him invalided out of the last two races with back injuries. Piquet took the title, but at least Mansell could look back on another electrifyingly successful season which included an even more memorable second British Grand Prix victory, earned after he outfumbled Nelson in a sensational overtaking manoeuvre at Silverstone's super-fast Stowe corner on the penultimate lap of the race!

Sadly, the political climate between Williams and Honda had become frosty, to say the least, resulting in a termination of the Anglo-Japanese alliance at the end of the '87 season.

Some ten months later, frustrated with the endless problems he had encountered with the Judd V8-engined Williams FW12, Mansell announced that he was, after all, switching to Ferrari for the 1989 season. The tantalising prospect of following in the footsteps of Mike Hawthorn, Peter Collins and John Surtees as 'an Englishman at Maranello' clearly seemed irresistible.

The Italian cars might have been less than totally competitive over the previous couple of seasons, but Nigel understandably held out great hope for the new 3.5 litre V12-engined type 640, designed by the highly respected John Barnard, which was nearing completion for the new season.

From the outset, Mansell seemed more relaxed than ever, admitting that he was happy to escape the commitments to the multitude of Williams team sponsors in exchange for just Marlboro and Ferrari. Moreover, he would be regarded as a hero from the word go when he took the new Ferrari 640 to a lucky first time victory in the Brazilian Grand Prix. The car had been beset by so many mechanical problems throughout practice that he never believed it would last the distance.

Later that summer he added the Hungarian

THAT GLORIOUS MOMENT AT RIO IN 1989 WHEN HE WON ON HIS DEBUT OUTING WITH THE SUPERB FERRARI 640. FROM NOW ON, HE WOULD BE DEIFIED IN ITALY

MANSELL **TWENTYTHREE**

Grand Prix to his tally of victories, out-manoeuvring Ayrton Senna's McLaren-Honda brilliantly as they came up to lap a slower car. His domination of the Portuguese Grand Prix at Estoril came badly unravelled, however, when he overshot his pit on arriving for a routine tyre change.

Unthinkingly in the pressure of the moment, he failed to let his mechanics pull the car back into position, as permitted in the regulations. Instead, he flicked the Ferrari's semi-automatic trans-mission into reverse and backed up a few feet. He thus faced instant dis-qualification, but acceler-ated back onto the circuit.

The black flag was shown to him as he came up to pass Senna's McLaren-Honda, which was leading – but he was vehement that he didn't see it. He dived inside Senna going into the first cor-ner and the two cars collided, spinning off into the sand trap and out of the race. Not only was Nigel excluded from the results, but FISA suspended him from the following weekend's Spanish Grand Prix at Jerez. He threatened to retire. And in 1990 he faced even more potential opposition from within his new team for Gerhard Berger was leaving Ferrari to join McLaren – replacing Alain Prost. The Frenchman, having fallen out with Ayrton Senna, was now hot-footing it in the opposite direction.

The 1990 season was certain to be disap-pointing for Mansell. Prost triumphed in the second race of the season at São Paulo, coinci-dentally in Senna's backyard, and then went on to win the Mexican, French and British races in quick succession.

By the time he arrived at Silverstone Mansell was not totally certain he wanted to continue with Ferrari into 1991. Ferrari's president, Piero Fusaro, had spent much of the French Grand Prix weekend attempting to persuade him to renew his contract, but he was not convinced by these overtures.

He qualified brilliantly for pole position in front of his home crowd at Silverstone, lead-ing the British Grand Prix before gearchange trouble intervened and he retired, agonisingly with only nine laps to go.

At the time, it must have seemed a crushing disappointment and, shortly after the race, he made a firm declaration that he would retire at the end of the season. Now 36 years old, he had been slogging along the GP trail for a decade and seemed no nearer to securing that elusive World Championship.

'I'm not making an excuse, just a straight-forward statement,' he said. 'I have been thinking about this a lot over the last four months and it is not an emotional decision. The British Grand Prix seemed the most appropriate place to announce my decision.

'I am looking forward to putting my family first for the first time in my life. I am looking forward to racing hard to the end of the year, and if I can help Alain to win the champi-onship, and perhaps win a few races myself, then all to the good.

'I have nothing else to say. As of now the Australian Grand Prix in Adelaide will be my final race. I don't want to burst into tears in front of you, but this is the hardest decision of my life.'

At Monza he convened a personal press conference to reaffirm his decision to retire. Yet, less than a month later, he announced that he would be accepting an offer to return to the Williams camp.

'The response to my retirement from the fans, manufacturers, teams from many different formulae and the world's sports press was totally opposed to my decision, and I have been under severe pressure to reconsid-

MANSELL TWENTYFIVE

er ever since,' he said.

'I have been touched by the fantastic encouragement from not only the British but fans all round the world for me to continue in F1.'

As team leader, Mansell's continual cajoling would be a key factor behind the development of the splendid new Williams-Renault FW14 into a consistently competitive force. Despite failing to score any points until the fourth race of the season, when Nigel took a strong second place at Monaco to Senna's McLaren-Honda, he gradually whittled away the Brazilian's early lead in the drivers' World Championship.

A splendid succession of mid-season victories at Magny-Cours, Silverstone and Hockenheim seriously built up the momentum of Mansell's title challenge. Disappointingly, a key retirement in the Belgian Grand Prix at Spa and subsequent disqualification at Estoril following a fumbled tyre change left Nigel with only an outside chance of championship glory as the team went into the penultimate race of the year, the Japanese Grand Prix at Suzuka.

MANSELL IN RELAXED 1991 MOOD. THIS WAS THE YEAR WHEN HE WAS RUNNER-UP IN THE TITLE CHASE FOR THE THIRD TIME

On this occasion, McLaren and Honda had every-thing taped at the front of the field and Mansell's title hopes ended ignominiously in a sand trap after he spun off challenging Senna for second place. Ayrton and McLaren had got away by the skin of their teeth – and they knew it. Mansell was runner-up in the championship for the third time in his career, but nobody could be left underestimating the potential strength of the Williams-Renault challenge for 1992. The rest, as they say, is history...

Away from the circuits Nigel Mansell's burning desire to be a winner spills over into all his other sporting activities. He took up golf in the wake of his 1977 Brands Hatch Formula Ford shunt and quickly reduced his handicap to single figures. A succession of pro-am tournaments over the years intensified his obsession with the game. He became great friends with Greg Norman – after

whom his second son was named – and was invited to play in the 1988 Australian Open. He found it something of a salutary experience and failed to make the cut.

'I would never do another tournament like that until I am much better,' he said. 'At one stage I was one under par, but I gripped the club so hard I hit the ball into the boonies and immediately went one over. The pressure is amazing! And the worst thing is that you're up there, out in front of everyone, without a helmet and mask to hide behind, on permanent display!'

Nigel Mansell never thought he would fail in his quest to make it to the top in his chosen sport. As Peter Windsor remembers: 'What you must understand about Nigel is that, after his first Formula 1 drive with Lotus in Austria, back in 1980, he came away absolutely knowing in his own mind that he was faster than the team's two regular drivers, Mario Andretti and Elio de Angelis.

'There was no shred of doubt in his mind.'

A SECOND PLACE
AT MONACO
(BELOW) GOT
MANSELL'S
1991 POINTS
SCORE OFF THE
GROUND

FRIENDSHIP WITH
GREG NORMAN
(ABOVE) LED TO AN
INVITATION FOR NIGEL
TO PLAY IN THE 1988
AUSTRALIAN OPEN
(LEFT)

MANSELL **TWENTYSEVEN**

1992 WORLD CHAMPION

NIGEL CONFERS WITH WILLIAMS TECHNICAL DIRECTOR PATRICK HEAD, ONE OF THE ARCHITECTS OF HIS CHAMPIONSHIP SUCCESS

ROUND 1: SOUTH AFRICAN GRAND PRIX, 1 MARCH

Five years after scoring only the second win of his Grand Prix career in the last South African Grand Prix to be held, Nigel Mansell returned to open his World Championship season on a spectacularly triumphant note at the extensively revised circuit near Johannesburg.

RACE RESULT	
1 NIGEL MANSELL	
2 RICCARDO PATRESE	
3 AYRTON SENNA	
4 MICHAEL SCHUMACHER	
5 GERHARD BERGER	
6 JOHNNY HERBERT	
WORLD CHAMPIONSHIP	
1 NIGEL MANSELL	10 PTS
2 RICCARDO PATRESE	6 PTS
3 AYRTON SENNA	4 PTS
4 MICHAEL SCHUMACHER	3 PTS
5 GERHARD BERGER	2 PTS
6 JOHNNY HERBERT	1 PT

F inally the speculation over. A winter's intensive testing coned once and for all to the history books, it now time for the Grand Prix teams and ers to stand up and be counted. And d Nigel Mansell possibly sustain the ning testing form of the superbly quick iams-Renault FW14B? Might Ferrari alise its challenge under the steward of Luca di Montezemolo? Would aren-Honda stay on top with Senna and er?

the basis of what we saw at Kyalami, answers to those questions were yes, no maybe, respectively. The new Williams ed devastatingly quick. Mansell was st in every one of the four timed practice

MANSELL TOOK THE WILLIAMS FW14B TO A CRUSHING DEBUT VICTORY IN SOUTH AFRICA

THE VIEW MANSELL GAVE THE OPPOSITION AT KYALAMI (ABOVE). FAR RIGHT: LOOKING NERVOUS DURING QUALIFYING

sessions, started from pole and looked in complete control throughout. The only blemish on that quite remarkable canvas came when he pirouetted into a sand trap on the outside of the right-hander before the pits on Saturday afternoon.

'I am pushing myself absolutely to the limit,' explained Mansell. 'That is probably part of the reason why I went off.' But he was quick to draw attention to the fact that reigning World Champion Ayrton Senna's McLaren-Honda MP4/6 – last year's car – was second on the grid, albeit 0.8 seconds away from his pole winning time.

It was difficult to get an accurate perspective from qualifying. Senna felt that he had quite a major performance deficit to make up, but was comforted by the thought that the new McLaren-Honda MP4/7 was in the pipeline. And there was strength in depth to the McLaren challenge, with Gerhard Berger third on the grid ahead of Riccardo Patrese in the other Williams-Renault FW14B.

Riccardo had suffered gearbox problems on Friday and difficulties setting the base-line

ride heights on the active suspension on Saturday. Come the race, however, things would be very different.

Mansell was worried only that things seemed to be going too well. But when the green light came on at the start he accelerated cleanly away from the pack as they crowded through the first right-hander with Patrese rocketing through from the second row, elbowing Senna aside, to slot the second Williams-Renault in tight on his tail.

Nigel led every one of the 72 laps, popping in the fastest shortly before the end to underline his supremacy. Riccardo, realising that he was not going to be able to hold Nigel, wisely concentrated on driving just fast enough to keep second place out of Senna's clutches, while the Brazilian tried to keep as much pressure on the second Williams as he could. But he conceded that didn't amount to much.

'I couldn't really see how it would be possible to overtake him,' said Ayrton, 'but I kept pressing hard thinking well, maybe he will be held up in traffic and I can get close

THE START OF SOMETHING BIG. NIGEL AND TEAM-MATE RICCARDO PATRESE ON THE VICTORY ROSTRUM AFTER THEIR 1-2 SUCCESS

enough to take advantage of it. But, really, there is no way we can fight with the Williams.'

Senna's third place was due reward for a characteristically dogged performance, while young German Michael Schumacher performed splendidly in the Benetton-Ford B191B to split Ayrton from Berger in fifth place. The top six was completed by the talented young Englishman Johnny Herbert in the Lotus 102D.

At the end of the afternoon everybody simply stood around wondering whether this was a freak result or a portent of things to come. With both Ferraris retiring with engine problems, the opposition seemed, by and large, to have neither the speed nor the reliability to present much of a threat.

Senna summed up his personal feelings: 'Right now I don't think we (McLaren) have a car that can win. Williams and Renault have a better package and Nigel and Riccardo deserved to finish first and second.'

Nigel, however, was more cautious and sought to underplay his apparent advantage. 'I don't think we've got a great advantage, though,' he responded. 'I can remember a lot of races last year where Ayrton won by a long way. But I will say that Renault and Elf have found us a lot more horsepower over the winter and the Williams team have done a good, solid job.'

They also came away from Kyalami with 16 championship points in the bag. Time alone would tell the rest.

ROUND 2: MEXICAN GRAND PRIX, 22 MARCH

Over the bumps and ripples of Mexico City's Autodromo Hermanos Rodriguez, the Williams-Renault battlewagon rolled triumphantly onwards. Mansell and Patrese monopolised the front row of the grid, but this time it was Benetton which proved the 'best of the rest' rather than McLaren.

The strongest card in Mansell's hand seemed, on the face of it, to be the computer-controlled reactive suspension on the Williams-Renault FW14B, but Nigel and team-mate Riccardo Patrese reported that it seemed to make little difference over the notorious corrugated surface of the Mexican track. Even Williams technical director Patrick Head admitted that the team had been a little worried that the reactive suspension computer software might not be able to keep up with all the bumps. But it got the job done.

during the Saturday untimed session, so he switched to the spare car at the start of second qualifying only to lose 20 minutes with computer failure.

Third and fourth places on the grid fell to the Benettons of Michael Schumacher and Martin Brundle, with the McLaren-Hondas of Gerhard Berger and Ayrton Senna trailing fifth and sixth. As far as Ayrton was concerned, he was fortunate to be starting the race at all.

On Friday afternoon he lost control on a fast ess-bend and slammed heavily into the retaining wall. A front suspension link pushed through the chassis and left him in acute pain with what he thought was a broken leg. Happily, it was only badly bruised and he was able to take part in second qualifying. Berger also crashed heavily on Saturday, but was thankfully unhurt.

Throughout race morning the ambient temperature continued to rise relentlessly, triggering worries in some people's minds about possible tyre wear problems. Mansell himself came to the grid in a slightly concerned state, worried about sudden oversteer which seemed to have developed on the warm-up lap. He made some last minute changes to the chassis set-up before the grid was cleared, and kept his fingers firmly crossed.

Using the Williams FW14B's sophisticated traction control system to minimise wheelspin in second and third gears on the long run down to the first corner, Mansell proved that he had little to worry about. With Patrese in his wake, the Englishman seized the initiative from the outset, with the bruised and battered Senna making an audacious bid to take third place as they jostled into the braking zone.

Further back, Ivan Capelli's Ferrari collided with Karl Wendlinger's March as they accelerated away from the starting grid, both men being eliminated on the spot, and there was more drama as Herbert spun his Lotus at the first turn, forcing Andrea de Cesaris's Tyrrell into some pretty dramatic avoiding action. 'My fault – what a wally!' shrugged Johnny, with admirable candour.

Mansell was over a second ahead at the end of the first lap, extending his advantage

MANSELL AND PATRESE BEAT McLAREN AND BENETTON TO THE FIRST CORNER (LEFT). BELOW: THE QUIETLY CONFIDENT LOOK OF A WINNER

Nigel produced another dominant performance to throw pole position beyond challenge during Friday's qualifying session, but Riccardo was quickest on Saturday, even though he was unable to match the Englishman's best. Nigel's race car suffered engine problems

**THIS TIME SCHU-
MACHER JOINED
NIGEL AND
RICCARDO ON
THE ROSTRUM,
CHEERED ON BY
THE PASSIONATE
LOCALS (RIGHT)**

to 2.1 seconds on lap two and then became embroiled with his team-mate in a contest for fastest lap. Back and forth went the initiative between Nigel and Riccardo, but eventually the Italian developed a slight blister on his left-front tyre and began to drop away. Mansell had again won the day in decisive style.

Thereafter Nigel dominated the race to win by just over 13 seconds, while Schumacher outran Berger for the second successive race.

This time the young German claimed the first podium finish of his career with a strong third place. Martin Brundle also proved his quality by briefly getting the upper hand in a wheel-to-wheel battle with Gerhard's McLaren, only to be forced into retirement with severe engine overheating.

For Senna, early retirement with gearchange troubles must have come as a welcome relief from his discomfort, but it seemed as though the McLaren team was locked into a worryingly uncompetitive trend with its old car. The top six was rounded off by de Cesaris, who had recovered from his Tyrrell's inadvertent first lap excursion in masterly style, while this time Lotus's single point for sixth place went the way of Mika Häkkinen, who led Herbert across the line.

Could Nigel imagine a better start to the 1992 season than two victories? 'Yes, three wins,' he replied, deadpan. Clearly, he was getting a taste for this sustained level of success!

MANSELL **THIRTYFOUR**

RACE RESULT		
1	NIGEL MANSELL	
2	RICCARDO PATRESE	
3	MICHAEL SCHUMACHER	
4	GERHARD BERGER	
5	ANDREA DE CESARIS	
6	MIKA HÄKKINEN	
WORLD CHAMPIONSHIP		
1	NIGEL MANSELL	20 PTS
2	RICCARDO PATRESE	12 PTS
3	MICHAEL SCHUMACHER	7 PTS
4	GERHARD BERGER	5 PTS
5	AYRTON SENNA	4 PTS
6	ANDREA DE CESARIS	2 PTS

ROUND 3: BRAZILIAN GRAND PRIX, 5 APRIL

Despite the presence of a brand new McLaren in the ranks of the opposition, Nigel Mansell made it three in a row by notching up victory at São Paulo's challenging Interlagos circuit. But it was not all plain sailing for the Englishman. This time teammate Riccardo Patrese led from the start and Nigel had to use every ounce of his strategy to get ahead...

RACE RESULT	
1	NIGEL MANSELL
2	RICCARDO PATRESE
3	MICHAEL SCHUMACHER
4	JEAN ALESI
5	IVAN CAPELLI
6	MICHELE ALBORETO

WORLD CHAMPIONSHIP		
1	NIGEL MANSELL	30 PTS
2	RICCARDO PATRESE	18 PTS
3	MICHAEL SCHUMACHER	11 PTS
4	GERHARD BERGER	5 PTS
5	AYRTON SENNA	4 PTS
6	JEAN ALESI	3 PTS

Nigel Mansell's confidence seemed to be surging to fresh heights each time he strapped himself into the cockpit of his Williams-Renault FW14B. In stiflingly sunny conditions, he started the first qualifying session at Interlagos just as he meant to go on. On his third flying lap he took pole position – with a lap which, at the time, was a remarkable 3.3 seconds faster than any other car on the 2.687-mile circuit!

MANSELL ACKNOWLEDGES ANOTHER WIN (RIGHT), AND THE WILLIAMS FW14B (BELOW) REMAINS UNBEATEN

'It was a special lap,' admitted Nigel with a degree of understatement. 'When you go through the fast corners and then analyse it, you ask yourself whether you could have gone any quicker. I could not have gone quicker. It was really nice and satisfying. That's when you know you've done a really hot lap.

'You know that even given another 100 times and another 100 sets of tyres, you could not have gone quicker.'

It was a performance which certainly got the attention of Ayrton Senna in the Brazilian's personal backyard. In an effort to respond to the Williams-Renault challenge, the McLaren team had decided, even before Kyalami, to bring forward the race debut of its new 1992 car, the MP4/7A, from its originally intended maiden outing in Spain a month later. It made little difference to the overall picture.

Although Senna would qualify the new car admirably in third place, he was still a depressing 2.2 seconds slower than Mansell's pole time and 1.8 seconds away from Patrese in second place. In fact, the closest he got to Mansell all weekend came in the closing moments of second qualifying when, due to a misunderstanding between the two men, Nigel slid off into the retaining wall and was lucky to escape with bruising and slight concussion.

Gerhard Berger wound up third on the grid, followed by Michael Schumacher's Benetton, Jean Alesi's Ferrari F92A and Martin Brundle's Benetton.

On the face of it, Nigel would now be able to enjoy another trouble-free run to victory, but Riccardo clearly had other ideas and made a perfectly timed getaway on the green light to lead Mansell into the first corner. At the bottom of the hill beyond that first chicane, Nigel attempted to dive down the inside – only for Patrese to slam the door firmly in his face.

'I think that was one of the worst starts ever,' said Mansell, 'and in the end I was pleased that I didn't stall the engine and just managed to get going!' Now he was going to have his work very clearly cut out to catch the on-form Patrese, who was absolutely determined to capitalise on this unexpected advantage.

While the two Williams-Renaults stormed

SECOND QUALIFYING SAW MANSELL SURVIVE A COLLISION WITH THE WALL (RIGHT) FOLLOWING A BRUSH WITH SENNA

away at the head of the pack, Senna's new McLaren bottled up an increasingly frustrated bunch of rivals headed by Schumacher's Benetton. Within a few laps the McLaren's Honda engine began to cut out intermittently, further slowing the Brazilian's progress. Schumacher in particular, not appreciating Senna's technical plight, came to the conclusion that Ayrton was simply messing everybody about – and made a pointed, public observation to that effect once the race was over!

Meanwhile, Mansell was trying every trick in the book to displace his team-mate, but Riccardo steadfastly refused to be rattled. It seemed that Nigel's only chance to reverse the Williams running order would come at the scheduled mid-race tyre stops.

Sure enough, Mansell stopped on lap 29 and his car was stationary for 8.5 seconds. On his return to the race on fresh tyres, by his own admission, he 'cheated' a little. 'I switched off the rev-limiter and drove two laps absolutely flat out at qualifying speed,' he grinned later. As a result, when Riccardo was briefly balked by slower cars on the lap before he came into the pits, Nigel had built up just sufficient additional momentum to shoot past into the lead while Patrese was still accelerating back down the pit lane.

From that point on, the outcome of the race was never in doubt. Mansell surged

FRANK WILLIAMS WATCHES IMPASSIVELY (RIGHT) AS NIGEL CELEBRATES VICTORY NUMBER THREE (FAR RIGHT)

onwards to a half-minute victory and nobody else was on the same lap as the victorious Williams-Renaults. Senna eventually retired, leaving Schumacher third ahead of Jean Alesi's Ferrari, which had earlier pushed Brundle's Benetton into the pit wall, with the similar car of Ivan Capelli in fifth. Michele Alboreto's Footwork-Mugen completed the top six.

'Riccardo drove really well,' said Mansell. 'He didn't make a single mistake that I saw and I was there for the whole time up to the pit stops. It was a big fight and a great race!'

MANSELL **THIRTYNINE**

Returning to Europe, Formula 1 exchanged the torrid heat of South America for the dank, overcast and rainy conditions of Barcelona's Circuit de Catalunya. But the fact that the rain in Spain fell mainly in the plain made little difference to Nigel Mansell. He never put a wheel wrong in truly atrocious conditions.

ROUND 4: SPANISH GRAND PRIX, 3 MAY

At the sharp end of the Spanish starting grid it was an undeniably familiar sight. Mansell was in pole position by a second, but the strength and consistency of Michael Schumacher's challenge could not be ignored. Now armed with the brand new Benetton B192, the young German survived several spins during practice to take second place on the grid – and his first front row start.

Ayrton Senna's McLaren MP4/7A lined up third, with Riccardo Patrese an unaccustomed fourth. He had been unhappy with his car's performance during Friday's dry quali-

fying session and Saturday's monsoon had wiped out any prospect of his registering an improvement.

The opposition was beginning to feel guardedly confident about the prospect of chipping away at the Williams team's advantage. Schumacher grinned broadly at his own personal achievement and even Senna seemed hopeful. 'If it rains,' he mused, 'I think we will be able to achieve a good position. But if it is dry, our results will probably be more discreet.' His voice trailed away slightly.

Ivan Capelli and Jean Alesi, who qualified their Ferraris fifth and eighth, separated by Gerhard Berger's McLaren and Martin Brundle's Benetton, were also particularly upbeat and optimistic about the prospect of a wet race. Indeed, when the green light signalled the start in torrential conditions, Alesi demonstrated that Ferrari also has an excellent traction control system, by bursting through to take an initial third place behind

RACE RESULT

1	NIGEL MANSELL	
2	MICHAEL SCHUMACHER	
3	JEAN ALESI	
4	GERHARD BERGER	
5	MICHELE ALBORETO	
6	PIERLUIGI MARTINI	

WORLD CHAMPIONSHIP

1	NIGEL MANSELL	40 PTS
2	RICCARDO PATRESE	18 PTS
3	MICHAEL SCHUMACHER	17 PTS
4	GERHARD BERGER	8 PTS
5	JEAN ALESI	7 PTS
6	AYRTON SENNA	4 PTS

MANSELL KEPT COMMAND (LEFT) IN THE MOST ATROCIOUS CONDITIONS TO NOTCH UP HIS FOURTH WIN OF THE YEAR. INSET, WAITING FOR THE OFF

to a wet set-up,' explained Mansell, 'because there was always a chance that conditions might dry out, so a compromise set-up was the way to go.

'We also found ourselves with slightly too little wing angle for the conditions and were carrying perhaps slightly more fuel than we needed for a wet race. In the circumstances, though, it was unavoidable and I'm sure other people had similar problems.'

Indeed they did, although the most over-whelming problem would be keeping pace with Mansell's Williams. On lap 20 the hith-erto unbroken symmetry of Williams's 1992 results was blown apart when Patrese skat-ed off the road into one of the unyielding retaining walls. Momentarily wrong-footed by a slower car, Riccardo found himself on a particularly deep puddle, lost grip and slewed off the circuit.

His misfortune handed Schumacher a clear run at Mansell's leading Williams and, indeed, by lap 50 Nigel's advantage – once 21 seconds – had shrunk to less than 5 seconds. Young Schumacher admitted to being slightly confused!

'I was only really worrying about keeping ahead of Senna in third place,' he admitted, 'but then I saw Mansell. I just couldn't believe I was so close to him – I thought he must have spun!'

Mansell, who had been carving a very cir-cumspect path through the back-markers, immediately responded to this sudden chal-lenge and opened out his advantage to 16.6 seconds after 55 laps. Clearly, the Williams traction control system was working every bit as effectively as the Ferrari version!

Nigel duly reeled off the remaining rain-soaked laps to one of his finest ever victo-ries. A superb second place for Schumacher confirmed the young German's status as one of the sport's most glittering new stars, while Jean Alesi harried the McLarens to such excellent effect during his recovery drive that he not only overtook Berger but hustled Senna into a mistake, the Brazilian spinning into retirement with three laps to go.

It was Nigel's 25th career victory, equalling the achievements of Jim Clark and Niki Lauda, as well as matching Jackie Stewart's record of three consecutive Grand Prix victories.

Mansell and Patrese. However, to several of his rivals, it seemed as though the little French-man's race had started fractionally before any-body else's!

Five laps into the race saw Mansell exert-ing a 4-second advantage over his team-mate, but Alesi was still holding off Schumacher in third place and the McLarens of Senna and Berger were next up, about to become embroiled in their own personal bat-tle. By lap ten Patrese was 13 seconds clear of the third-place man, which had now become Schumacher, Alesi dropping back into the clutches of Berger who nudged him into a quick spin at the first corner. In fact, Jean was not alone; cars were pirouetting in all directions.

Intriguingly, few competitors had opted for a 'full wet' chassis set-up, most preferring to hedge their bets. 'You couldn't really commit

With unchallenged and total assurance, Mansell ran out the winner in front of the Italian crowd at Imola, with Patrese resuming his customary role in his wake. In so doing, Nigel carved himself a slice of motor racing history as the only driver to date who has won the first five Grands Prix in a season.

ROUND 5: SAN MARINO GRAND PRIX, 17 MAY

He may no longer be a Ferrari driver, but Mansell still loves racing in Italy. Hailed as a conquering hero ever since winning his maiden Grand Prix in a Ferrari in 1989, his popularity has been undiminished by his switch back to the Williams squad. Mansell in the cockpit is every Italian motor

ACUTE CONCEN-TRATION FROM NIGEL AT THE START, REWARD-ED (BELOW) WITH A CLEAN AND EFFICIENT GETAWAY FROM POLE POSITION WITH PATRESE FALLING IN BEHIND

RACE RESULT	
1	NIGEL MANSELL
2	RICCARDO PATRESE
3	AYRTON SENNA
4	MARTIN BRUNDLE
5	MICHELE ALBORETO
6	PIERLUIGI MARTINI

WORLD CHAMPIONSHIP		
1	NIGEL MANSELL	50 PTS
2	RICCARDO PATRESE	24 PTS
3	MICHAEL SCHUMACHER	17 PTS
4	AYRTON SENNA	8 PTS
	GERHARD BERGER	8 PTS
6	JEAN ALESI	7 PTS

KITTED UP AND READY TO GO, MANSELL IMMERSES HIM-SELF IN HIS OWN PRIVATE THOUGHTS BEFORE THE START

racing enthusiast's cup of tea: dauntless, uncompromising, exciting.

On the face of it, Mansell had to work even harder than usual to exert an advantage over the new McLaren-Hondas. Senna challenged dramatically on Friday, briefly holding provisional pole position, but Nigel trumped his most dangerous rival with a time over a second quicker than the McLaren team leader.

'It was a perfect lap,' enthused Mansell. 'I was ready for it; the tyres came in at just the right moment and, most importantly of all, I had no traffic.

'But it has been like musical chairs today. I qualified my race car with the race engine – the RS3C. The new RS4 was in my spare car which I let Riccardo qualify and I think he did a great job considering the time he had.'

That said, Mansell warned that McLaren seemed to be pressing hard. 'We urgently need the new Williams FW15. Another couple of races and we will be behind,' he predicted. This was an unduly pessimistic viewpoint.

Patrese was unlucky enough to suffer an electrical problem during the Friday morning free practice session. Although he switched to the spare, it was undergoing an engine change and he only got out with five minutes left, so he had to be content with fifth fastest place overnight. On Saturday he improved to take second place on the grid, but Nigel retained pole thanks to his efforts the previous afternoon.

The race took place in torrid conditions and the drivers' patience was not helped when the start was postponed for five minutes

after Karl Wendlinger stalled his March on the grid. At the green light Mansell was first away, but for a few fleeting seconds it seemed as though Senna would split the Williams-Renault duo on the jostling run down to the Tosa hairpin. Riccardo just squeezed through ahead, however, and the format of the race was firmly established.

Coming into the downhill Rivazza left-hander at the end of the opening lap, Berger hurtled past Michael Schumacher's Benetton to take fourth place, so they came past the pits at the end of the opening lap in best Noah's Ark fashion. Mansell and Patrese were already inching away with McLaren (Senna and Berger) and Benetton (Schumacher and Brundle) leading the chase.

Things began to look ominous for the Ferrari fans when Ivan Capelli locked up his brakes and slid into the sand trap at the Acque Minerale chicane, leaving only Jean Alesi's car in business. But the doughty young Frenchman was taking a leaf out of Mansell's book when it came to sheer determination, opting to run non-stop on a single set of tyres.

Patrese and Mansell made their routine tyre stops on laps 19 and 23 respectively without their positions being jeopardised. For a few laps after Nigel's return to the circuit, the two Williams-Renaults were separated by only a couple of seconds. But then Mansell resumed his high speed rhythm and eased away again to win by a whisker under 10 seconds.

Third place fell to a hard-driving Senna and, after Berger and Alesi were eliminated in a territorial dispute at the Tosa hairpin, Martin Brundle scored his first points of the season with fourth place for Benetton. Martin had raced with terrific verve and kept ahead of team-mate Michael Schumacher on this occasion, until the young German driver spun into the tyre barrier at Rivazza, damaging his mount beyond repair.

Michele Alboreto's Footwork and Pierluigi Martini's Dallara-Ferrari completed the top six, their worthy achievements

NIGEL ACCELERATES HIS WILLIAMS-RENAULT FW14B OUT OF THE PIT LANE AT THE START OF IMOLA QUALIFYING

but a footnote to Mansell's overwhelming success at the front of the field. The end of the race saw Senna exhausted and wracked with upper body cramps which left him slumped in the cockpit of his McLaren for almost twenty minutes after he'd passed the chequered flag.

Mansell and Patrese were thus alone on the victory rostrum, every bit as unchallenged as they had been out on the circuit.

HE MAY NOW BE
IN A WILLIAMS,
BUT THE
EMOTIONAL
ITALIAN FANS
STILL REGARD
NIGEL AS ONE OF
THEIR GREAT
FERRARI HEROES

ROUND 6: MONACO GRAND PRIX, 31 MAY

Nigel's Monaco jinx struck yet again. On this epic street circuit, where he had first led a Grand Prix eight years before, Mansell qualified brilliantly on pole position and seemed set fair for a clear-cut victory. But a loose rear wheel forced him to make a late race pit stop and he dropped to second behind Ayrton Senna's McLaren.

MANSELL
LOOKED A
CERTAIN
WINNER UNTIL
BAD LUCK
INTERVENED
AND HANDED
THE RACE TO
SENNA

igel Mansell
was shatter-
ingly quick at Monaco during qualifying and
the second timed session through the streets
of the Principality was highlighted by a dramatic battle for pole position between him
and team-mate Riccardo Patrese. Four times
during that frenetic final hour they traded
fastest lap and, although Riccardo seemed
capable of countering anything Nigel did,
somehow one just knew that the Englishman
had something special up his sleeve.

Sure enough, he eventually plucked out a
best time an incredible 0.9 seconds faster
than Patrese, leaving onlookers rocking on
their heels in disbelief. Third on the grid was
the irrepressible Senna, then Jean Alesi's
Ferrari, Gerhard Berger in the other
McLaren-Honda and Michael Schumacher's
Benetton B192.

That wasn't to say Mansell's two days of
qualifying had been totally without their hic-
cups. In the first qualifying session he'd had
a big spin coming down into the waterfront
chicane.

'It's a bit of a problem when you arrive at
the chicane backwards, heading into the sea
wall,' recounted Nigel. 'I dropped the clutch
and thought "the impact is going to happen
any minute". Then the car went sideways,
spun through 360 degrees and I carried on
going the way I was. I was lucky not to hit
the wall!'

Come the race, Mansell seemed set for his
sixth successive victory. The green light saw
him make a perfect getaway as the pack
sprinted for the uphill right-hander at Ste

MANSELL FORTYEIGHT

O NEAR AND
YET SO FAR.
LEFT: MANSELL
TAILS SENNA
PAST THE
CHEQUERED
G. INSET: AS
T WAS MEANT
TO BE AS NIGEL
DISAPPEARS IN
THE OPENING
STAGES

MANSELL FORTYNINE

Devote. But in those opening seconds of the race the most crucial element in losing Nigel his victory fell into place. From the second row, Senna launched his McLaren down the inside of Patrese and just squeezed in

between the Williams-Renaults as they went through the corner.

Nigel was to have no protective buffer. Not that it seemed he needed it in the early stages, of course, as he steadily eased away from the hard-driving Brazilian. Patrese, frustrated by lack of rear-end grip, dropped back into the clutches of Alesi and Schumacher. After Michael had dealt with the Italian car by bumping it badly enough to inflict long-term damage on the electronic controls for its semi-automatic gearbox, Riccardo spent most of the race giving the Benetton youngster a valuable lesson in overtaking problems at Monaco.

Mansell, meanwhile, hauled steadily away into the distance, stabilising his advantage first at 20 seconds and then extending it to 30. He was aided by Senna having to brake momentarily to avoid Michele Alboreto's Footwork which was manoeuvring back into action after a spin at Mirabeau.

Just when it looked as though it was all

over bar the shouting, Mansell suddenly felt his Williams twitch sideways in the tunnel on lap 71. He radioed that he was coming in for tyres – and it wasn't a particularly slick stop. And, as he accelerated back into the fray, Senna surged across the startline to take the lead.

On lap 72 Ayrton led the Williams by 5.1 seconds, but the Brazilian's tyres were badly worn and Nigel was revelling in the grip afforded by fresh rubber. Next time round it was 4.3 seconds, but Mansell carved two whole seconds out of his advantage with three laps to go. Surely Senna would not be able to hold on?

Yet, despite Nigel bobbing around frantically in the McLaren's wake, Senna refused to yield, covering Mansell's every move. On the last lap Nigel realised that, realistically, there was nothing more to be done. He settled for second place, unwilling to risk his certain six points in a win-or-bust effort. It was absolutely the right strategy.

'Coming through the tunnel in the lead,' I almost lost it,' explained Nigel, 'and we had a slightly longer pit stop than usual. When I saw Ayrton go by I knew we'd probably lost it. Up to then I had the race under control, but Ayrton was very fair and entitled to drive as he did. He made his car very wide!'

The problem was almost certainly a slightly loose wheel retaining nut, Patrick Head confirming that Nigel made exactly the right decision coming in when he did rather than staying out and risking an accident. Riccardo was third ahead of Schumacher with Martin Brundle's Benetton and Bertrand Gachot's Venturi-Lamborghini completing the list of points scorers.

MANSELL *FIFTYONE*

AWAITING THE START OF WHAT TURNED OUT TO BE A FATEFUL RACE (RIGHT). FRANK WILLIAMS (INSET) DOES NOT LOOK IMPRESSED ABOUT THE OUTCOME

ROUND 7: CANADIAN GRAND PRIX, 14 JUNE

As the World Championship battle made a return trip across the Atlantic, for the Canadian race at Montreal, it seemed as though Mansell's concern about the strengthening challenge from the new McLaren-Honda was quite valid. After running quickly enough to score a victory at Nigel's expense in Monaco, Senna proved that the low-down punch of the Honda V12 was just what was wanted for the two tight hairpins of the windswept circuit on Ile Notre Dame.

Friday qualifying saw Senna quickest from Patrese, Berger and Mansell, the Williams team leader complaining that his engine didn't feel as crisp as usual. 'I think this proves what I have been saying for some time,' observed Nigel, 'namely that the Honda engine is ahead on power.' It goes without saying that Senna didn't agree.

The weather forecast for the second day's qualifying did not look very promising. Sure enough, when Mansell took a first glance through his hotel window on Saturday morning the Montreal streets were glistening beneath a steady curtain of rain. It looked set for the day, but gradually it brightened up and the track dried progressively through the 90-minute free practice session.

Yet conditions in the afternoon were not quite ideal. Although Mansell improved to third, at Berger's expense, on this occasion Senna and Patrese remained beyond reach. On the third row of the grid were Michael Schumacher's Benetton and Johnny Herbert's promising Lotus 107, while row four contained Martin Brundle's Benetton and Jean Alesi's Ferrari. Mansell anticipated a hard race, but Senna believed it was an unrepresentative situation and that the

The worst race of Mansell's season. On lap 16 of the 69-lap event round Montreal's Circuit Gilles Villeneuve, Nigel pulled an overtaking manoeuvre on Ayrton Senna's leading McLaren which proved ambitious in the extreme and result-ed in him spinning out of the race. With Riccardo Patrese also failing to finish it was the first time in 1992 that both Williams drivers had retired.

MANSELL **FIFTYTHREE**

Williams was still quicker.

Nevertheless, overtaking would be next to impossible. At the start, Mansell strained every sinew to get ahead going into the first corner, but although he neatly cut out Patrese, there was no pressuring Ayrton. At the end of the first lap it was Senna, Mansell, Patrese, Berger, Schumacher, Brundle and the Lotus twins, Herbert and Mika Häkkinen, who made up the leading bunch. And nobody was getting away from anybody else.

Mansell would bring the Williams FW14B rushing up under Senna's rear wing as they braked for the two hairpins, but the Honda V12 launched the Brazilian out of those corners like a dragster. Even so, on lap 16, Nigel decided to launch an audacious assault on the lead.

Coming into the fast ess-bend before the pits, Williams number five jinked out of position and braked late on the inside line. It was also the dirty line. Senna didn't do Mansell any favours, but both Patrese and Berger, from their vantage points a few lengths back, deemed Nigel's challenge to be too ambitious.

Locking his brakes, Mansell found himself hurtling across the sandy apex before careering back onto the circuit beyond the chicane exit. Minus its nose wings and sundry bodywork, the car pirouetted to a halt as Senna went through still in the lead, Berger nipping past Patrese into what was now second place amid all the confusion.

For almost a lap, Nigel sat dazed in the cockpit. Then marshals assisted him over the wall into the pit lane. Bristling with indignation, he went straight over to berate McLaren boss Ron Dennis for what he regarded as Senna's rough driving. After a meeting with FISA permanent steward Peter Warr, he left the circuit without making an official protest.

Later Patrese would retire with

ANALYSING PRACTICE TIMES (INSET) WITH ROSANNE AND ENGINEER DAVID BROWN. IN EXTREMIS (MAIN PICTURE) DURING PRACTICE

gearchange problems, so it was left to Gerhard Berger's McLaren to come home the winner from Schumacher's Benetton, Senna having also failed to last the distance due to an electrical malfunction.

Mansell may, in fact, have been as much annoyed with himself as with the unfortunate circumstances of his retirement. As Patrese remarked with candour: 'He got off line, didn't have enough grip and couldn't make the corner. Ayrton didn't help him. He closed the door a little, but I don't think they touched.'

Frank Williams was more philosophical. 'Nigel didn't finish, nor did Ayrton,' he remarked. 'So we'll just have to consider it a draw.'

ROUND 8: FRENCH GRAND PRIX, 5 JULY

Striking French truck drivers hogged the headlines at the Circuit de Nevers as Mansell took to the track to set fastest time in the first qualifying session. The French chaos, with hundreds of road blocks all over the country, left many people wondering whether the cars would be able to get back for the big day of Nigel's year, the following weekend's British Grand Prix at Silverstone.

Back in Europe and back in front! That was the story of Nigel Mansell's second straight French Grand Prix win, but he had to battle harder than usual with Riccardo before a rain shower caused the race to be red-flagged. At the restart, Patrese didn't choose to make a fight of it and Mansell stormed away to equal Jackie Stewart's tally of 27 career victories.

MANSELL AND FW14B (LEFT) THIS TIME
FACED STERN OPPOSITION FROM TEAM-
MATE PATRESE. ABOVE: STORMY WEATHER.
BEFORE THE RAIN SHOWER WHICH
INTERRUPTED THE RACE

IN CONFERENCE WITH FORMER TRIPLE WORLD CHAMPION NIKI LAUDA (ABOVE). RIGHT: BREATHE IN! MANSELL IN THE RESTRICTED CONFINES OF THE WILLIAMS-RENAULT COCKPIT

Effectively trapped in a state of siege within the paddock at Magny-Cours, it remained to be seen whether or not the two dozen or so F1 transporters would be able to break out on Sunday night and make a dash for the Channel ports.

Much as this problem occupied some minds, Mansell was concentrating his efforts on buttoning up another pole position. He had a few engine problems on Friday which resulted in his swapping back and forth between the race car and spare, fitted respectively with RS4 and RS3C versions of the Renault V10 engine. Nigel also managed a brief off-track excursion on Saturday morning when, by his own admission, he got his feet tangled up in the pedals.

Mansell was also manifestly unimpressed

OVERHEAD SHOT
EMPHASISES
ULTRA-SLIM
PROFILE OF
MANSELL'S
WILLIAMS-RENAULT
FW14B CHASSIS

RACE RESULT		
1	NIGEL MANSELL	
2	RICCARDO PATRESE	
3	MARTIN BRUNDLE	
4	MIKA HÄKKINEN	
5	ERIK COMAS	
6	JOHNNY HERBERT	
WORLD CHAMPIONSHIP		
1	NIGEL MANSELL	66 PTS
2	RICCARDO PATRESE	34 PTS
3	MICHAEL SCHUMACHER	26 PTS
4	AYRTON SENNA	18 PTS
	GERHARD BERGER	18 PTS
6	JEAN ALESI	11 PTS

MANSELL **SIXTY**

by a not-so-subtle reference from McLaren team chief Ron Dennis as to what he regarded as the Englishman's inconsistent form. 'Under normal circumstances,' said Dennis, 'I would say we had no chance of the championship, but we're not facing normal circumstances. There is an emotional inconsistency in the performance of other teams.'

Mansell took the bait and fired back: 'He can say what he likes, it doesn't bother me. He's as jealous as hell. It's good to see them rattled. They were on top of the world for four years and they don't like it now that Williams and Renault are ahead.'

Patrese qualified second, with the McLaren-Hondas of Ayrton Senna and Gerhard Berger making up row two and Michael Schumacher's Benetton-Ford ahead of Jean Alesi's Ferrari on row three.

At the start, Riccardo made it clear that he had his own agenda. He launched straight into the lead and, after only four laps, had built up a 1.5-second lead over Mansell. Senna was eliminated when Schumacher rammed him on the opening lap, while Berger's distant challenge from third place evaporated when his car suffered engine failure after 11 laps.

On lap 16 a few spots of rain could be felt and Mansell really began to pressure Patrese. Then out came the red flag and everybody trickled back to the starting grid. Senna, by now out of the equation, gave Schumacher something of a lecture about first lap etiquette while Williams technical

TWO BRITS OUT OF THREE! MARTIN BRUNDLE JOINS MANSELL AND PATRESE ON THE ROSTRUM FOR THE FIRST TIME IN HIS CAREER

director Patrick Head had a word with Patrese, the result of which was Riccardo leading the first lap of the restart and then waving Mansell ahead.

Was he subjected to team orders? 'I have no comment to make on that,' said Patrese icily at the post-race press conference. Head clarified the situation. 'In the interval between the two parts of the race I told Riccardo that he was free to defend his position as long as it didn't unnecessarily jeopardise the safety of the cars.'

Either way, Patrese was going to be no threat to Nigel. The championship leader stamped his mastery on the race by forging ahead to win without challenge as the circuit was drenched by torrential rain in the closing stages.

Behind Patrese, Martin Brundle scored the best result of his career with a fine third for Benetton, his first visit to the Grand Prix rostrum. The Lotus 107s of Mika Häkkinen and Johnny Herbert finished fourth and sixth, sandwiching Eric Comas's Ligier, in what was the best possible curtain raiser for the British Grand Prix.

Happily, no outside influences did threaten the British round of the World Championship. The transporters duly left Magny-Cours without problem and made it to the Channel ports unmolested by striking truck drivers.

Nigel Mansell was now poised for possibly the most memorable weekend of his entire career.

Amid scenes more reminiscent of Monza or Le Mans, race fans flooded the circuit in a state of frenzied hysteria after Nigel Mansell simply upped and ran away with the British Grand Prix in breathtakingly dominant style. It was an epic example of a top driver extracting the maximum from the best car in the business – and Nigel's fifth F1 victory on his home turf.

ROUND 9: BRITISH GRAND PRIX, 12 JULY

BIG SHOT! MANSELL CELEBRATES HIS HOME VICTORY IN THE TRADITIONAL MANNER. INSET, GETTING AROUND THE PADDOCK ON TWO WHEELS

A s usual, Nigel, Rosanne, Chloe, Leo and Greg all stayed in their own caravan in a compound behind the paddock, soaking up the Silverstone atmosphere without the need to get in the helicopter queue every morning. At the pre-race tyre test Nigel had stunned the opposition with a best lap of 1m 20.56s and now he seemed certain to duplicate that achievement.

As things transpired, Friday's qualifying session at Silverstone would be the one that mattered, rain precluding all chance of

MANSELL SIXTYTHREE

improvement on Saturday. Mansell set the ball rolling with a 1m 20.503s, then a 1m 19.711s, an average speed of 146.66 mph. He retired to the pits and then emerged again to trim his time further to 1m 19.630s (146.81 mph). With 30 minutes of the hour-long session completed, he was down to 1m 9.161s. Surely that was enough?

OFF TO WORK WE GO. NIGEL PUTS HIS BEST FOOT FORWARD (RIGHT) AS HE CLIMBS INTO THE COCKPIT OF HIS WILLIAMS-RENAULT

No way. With just under ten minutes left he produced a 1m 18.965s to leave his supporters screaming with delight, the public enclosures a sea of Union Jack flags. He was on pole by the massive margin of 1.9 seconds ahead of Riccardo, an

THE WINNING NUMBER: MANSELL'S 'RED FIVE'

NIGEL HAS ALWAYS BEEN ABLE TO RELY ON OVERWHELMING SUPPORT AT SILVERSTONE FROM FANS WHO HAVE FOLLOWED HIS CAREER FROM THE START

achievement only partly due to the use of a special qualifying engine rumoured to employ variable length induction trumpets. It was a simply momentous achievement.

Ayrton Senna squeezed every ounce of potential from his McLaren-Honda to take third place on the grid ahead of leading regulars Michael Schumacher (Benetton-Ford), Gerhard Berger (McLaren-Honda) and Martin Brundle (Benetton-Ford). In Saturday morning's free practice session Patrese tangled with Erik Comas's Ligier in the Vale, crashing heavily and writing off the FW14B monocoque. That meant the Williams team had to build up a new car for the Italian to race and, by the time he took his place on the grid, he was still feeling

MANSELL **SIXTYSEVEN**

bruised and careworn.

Nevertheless, Riccardo got the jump on Mansell at the start, but Nigel sliced inside him on the short sprint between Copse and Becketts. By Stowe Mansell was already ten lengths clear of his team-mate and, as the sleek multi-coloured Williams carrying 'red five' on its nose cone catapulted out of Woodcote to complete the first lap, he was an amazing 3.2 seconds clear!

In successive laps his advantage was respectively 5.9, 7.9, 11.2 and on to an amazing 19.7 seconds after ten laps. Behind Patrese, Brundle had launched himself straight into third place from the start, and with Johnny Herbert's Lotus sixth behind Senna and Schumacher it was certainly a great day for British fans.

Mansell had once again confirmed that Silverstone was his own personal fiefdom. By lap 25 he was 34 seconds ahead of the pack and operating with such serene confidence that there was no trace of panic among the Williams team when he came in for fresh tyres, a leisurely 11.71-second stop, at the end of lap 30.

LONER. NIGEL DESTROYED HIS OPPOSITION AT SILVERSTONE IN A MANNER SELDOM EQUALLED BY ANY OF HIS RIVALS

Nigel was accelerating back down the pit lane on his fresh rubber even before Riccardo appeared out of Woodcote. The Goodyear engineers examined the tyres which had come off Nigel's car and advised Williams that they could signal Patrese to keep going. There was no wear problem at all.

The circuit organisers had been well aware that a track invasion was likely in the event of the almost inevitable Mansell victory. But even their well-laid plans could not have anticipated the hysterical reaction, thousands of fans spilling onto the track almost before Nigel had taken the chequered flag. He was swamped by his supporters before the end of his slowing-down lap and had to be rescued by officials.

Patrese was second, ahead of the magnificent Brundle who had kept Senna at bay for most of the race, the Brazilian retiring shortly before the end. Berger's McLaren then blew up on the run-in to the flag, allowing Schumacher through to fourth, while

RACE RESULT	
1	NIGEL MANSELL
2	RICCARDO PATRESE
3	MARTIN BRUNDLE
4	MICHAEL SCHUMACHER
5	GERHARD BERGER
6	MIKA HÄKKINEN

WORLD CHAMPIONSHIP		
1	NIGEL MANSELL	76 PTS
2	RICCARDO PATRESE	40 PTS
3	MICHAEL SCHUMACHER	29 PTS
4	GERHARD BERGER	20 PTS
5	AYRTON SENNA	18 PTS
6	MARTIN BRUNDLE	13 PTS

JOY UNCON-
FINED: ON THE
WINNERS' ROS-
TRUM FOR THE
FIFTH TIME IN HIS
HOME COUNTRY

Johnny Herbert's fine run ended with his Lotus jammed in gear. To round off the day, Williams test driver Damon Hill squeezed onto the back of the grid in his uncompetitive Brabham-Judd and was still plodding gallantly round at the finish.

In all the jubilation, it would have been nice if Mansell could have found time for a gentle word of admonishment to his overzealous supporters. But he declined to condemn the crowd.

'I'm not going to knock them,' he said. 'In a way I would like to compliment them. I think today has been the most wonderful day for the sport in the history of F1 at Silverstone.'

Well, yes and no. Everybody knew what Mansell meant; it was just a shame that the reckless minority had brought the British Grand Prix to the very brink of catastrophe.

And so to Hockenheim, the race at which Mansell had come closest to taking the World Championship points lead twelve months before. This time, although a puncture warning light forced Nigel into the pits early in the race, he resumed to overtake Ayrton Senna and equal the Brazilian's record of eight wins in a season.

ROUND 10: GERMAN GRAND PRIX, 28 JULY

Mansell was quickest in all four qualifying sessions, but an engine problem on Patrese's car meant that the Italian had to borrow Nigel's spare on Saturday afternoon, closing to within 0.4 seconds of his colleague to make certain of a front row starting position before spinning off in the stadium section.

Hockenheim had been partially resurfaced since the pre-race tyre test, as the reprofiled second chicane was deemed extremely unsatisfactory. Conditions were little improved and the track remained very bumpy at that point, claiming several casualties during the two days of practice.

Senna took the inside of the second row for McLaren after some dramatically spectacular motoring, while team-mate Berger made it an all red-and-white second row. A measure of how hard Senna was having to try in order to keep pace with the Williams-Renaults could be seen during the race morning warm-up when he spun violently over the high kerb on the right-hander before the start. The impact seriously damaged the underside of the chassis and forced him to take the spare McLaren for the race.

As at Silverstone, Patrese just got the edge on Mansell away from the grid, only to run slightly wide on the right-hander after the stadium. Nigel duly slipstreamed by on the race down to the first chicane to establish the team's customary symmetry at the head of the field. This was the order at the end of the opening lap, with Senna and Berger next up ahead of Schumacher and Brundle in

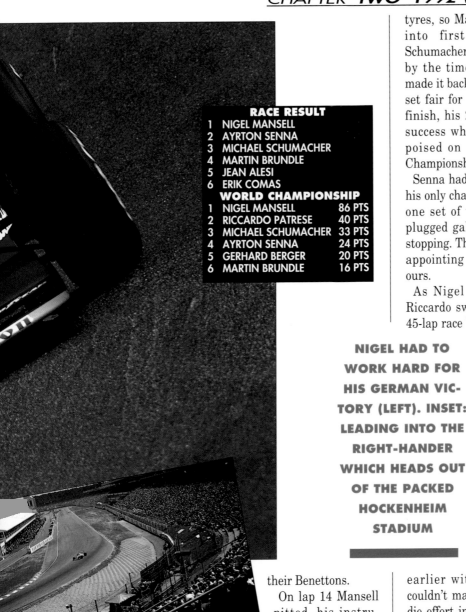

RACE RESULT		
1	NIGEL MANSELL	
2	AYRTON SENNA	
3	MICHAEL SCHUMACHER	
4	MARTIN BRUNDLE	
5	JEAN ALESI	
6	ERIK COMAS	
WORLD CHAMPIONSHIP		
1	NIGEL MANSELL	86 PTS
2	RICCARDO PATRESE	40 PTS
3	MICHAEL SCHUMACHER	33 PTS
4	AYRTON SENNA	24 PTS
5	GERHARD BERGER	20 PTS
6	MARTIN BRUNDLE	16 PTS

NIGEL HAD TO WORK HARD FOR HIS GERMAN VICTORY (LEFT). INSET: LEADING INTO THE RIGHT-HANDER WHICH HEADS OUT OF THE PACKED HOCKENHEIM STADIUM

tyres, so Mansell and Senna went through into first and second places with Schumacher also slipping ahead of Riccardo by the time the other Williams-Renault made it back onto the circuit. Now Nigel was set fair for a dominant run through to the finish, his 29th Grand Prix victory and a success which ensured he ended the day poised on the very brink of the World Championship.

Senna had already made up his mind that his only chance of success was to try making one set of tyres last to the finish, so he plugged gallantly on with no intention of stopping. This was destined to produce a disappointing outcome for Patrese's endeavours.

As Nigel extended his advantage, so Riccardo sweated through to lap 33 of the 45-lap race before he finally squeezed ahead of Schumacher into third place. This really meant that he would have to hurry if he was to catch Senna before the finish, although on fresh rubber it seemed like a quite feasible task.

In fact, it would end in disaster. As Nigel reeled off the few remaining laps to the chequered flag, without incident, Riccardo hauled himself right onto Senna's tail with three laps to go. Ayrton proved just as unyielding as he had been earlier with Mansell, and Patrese just couldn't make it through. In a final, do-or-die effort into the stadium on the final lap, Riccardo got off line on the dirt and spun ignominiously into retirement, to be classified eighth in the final order.

Afterwards Mansell reported that it had been a very difficult race and that he needed to see a dentist, such were the levels of his tyre vibration throughout the battle. He also said, yet again, that he was impressed by the power of the Honda V12 during the time he had been sitting behind Senna. It goes without saying, of course, that this was a view not mirrored by Ayrton.

On this occasion, however, the last comment on the race should be left to a dejected Riccardo Patrese. 'This was not the result I would have liked,' he said, with some understatement.

But Nigel Mansell came away from the German Grand Prix on top of the world. Well, four points away from the summit, at least!

their Benettons.

On lap 14 Mansell pitted, his instruments incorrectly signalling that he had a puncture, and by the time he resumed he was running third behind Patrese and Senna. Ayrton inwardly realised it was inevitable that he would eventually have to relinquish his place to the superior car/driver combination filling his mirrors, but that didn't mean he had to make life easy for Nigel. He fought tooth and nail to keep in front.

On lap 19 Nigel locked up going into the Ostkurve chicane, sliding straight on but fortunately missing the sand trap on the outside of the corner. Ironically, this slip enabled him to exit the corner slightly quicker and Ayrton, now facing the inevitable, signalled him through as they raced down to the following chicane.

At the end of that lap Patrese came in for

A hard-fought second place at the Hungaroring was good enough for Mansell to round off his great ambition and secure the World Championship, almost twelve years to the day since his F1 debut with a third Lotus in the 1980 Austrian Grand Prix. The race was won by Ayrton Senna, but only when Riccardo Patrese spun off after dominating the event from pole position.

PREPARING FOR
THE OFF:
MANSELL'S
WILLIAMS-
RENAULT IS
ROLLED OUT FOR
HIS MOST CRU-
CIAL RACE OF THE
SEASON

**WITH HELMET
FIRMLY ON,
NIGEL HAS A FEW
MOMENTS OF
PRIVACY ON A
WEEKEND WHICH
SAW HIM CON-
TINUALLY UNDER
THE SPOTLIGHT**

RACE RESULT

1	AYRTON SENNA
2	NIGEL MANSELL
3	GERHARD BERGER
4	MIKA HÄKKINEN
5	MARTIN BRUNDLE
6	IVAN CAPELLI

WORLD CHAMPIONSHIP

1	NIGEL MANSELL	92 PTS
2	RICCARDO PATRESE	40 PTS
3	AYRTON SENNA	34 PTS
4	MICHAEL SCHUMACHER	33 PTS
5	GERHARD BERGER	24 PTS
6	MARTIN BRUNDLE	18 PTS

NIGEL KEPT HIS NERVE TO FINISH SECOND, DESPITE DROPPING TO FOURTH AT THE FIRST CORNER (INSET) BEHIND PATRESE, SENNA AND BERGER

Nigel Mansell seemed surprisingly relaxed out of the cockpit throughout the Hungarian Grand Prix weekend. Perhaps it was the realisation that, even if he failed to clinch the title on this particular weekend, it could hardly remain out of his grasp for much longer. In any event, when Riccardo beat him to pole position for the first time this season he remained remarkably philosophical.

After what appeared to be a distinctly erratic performance, including a spin, on his final run round the tight, extremely slippery circuit near Budapest, Nigel radiated a relaxed serenity as he climbed from the

MANSELL **SEVENTYFIVE**

CHALLENGING
SENNA FOR
SECOND PLACE IN
THE EARLY
STAGES. BY
NOW, PATRESE IS
OUT OF SIGHT IN
THE LEAD

Williams and considered his position.

'I am on the front row of the grid, I have 46 points in hand over the opposition,' he smiled. 'Admittedly, I had a little problem which was totally my fault, pushing hard on tyres which were not fully warmed up. I have had an exciting day and I am just pleased to come through it all with a place on the front row.'

And did he feel under more pressure than usual? 'Not at all,' he replied. 'Quite the contrary, in fact. All I have to do this weekend is to drive for points.'

Mansell could afford to be philosophical. Provided that Patrese did not lead the race, a top three finish would be good enough. The two Williams-Renaults were comfortably ahead of their regular sparring partners, with Ayrton Senna's McLaren-Honda, Michael Schumacher's Benetton-Ford, Gerhard Berger's McLaren and the Ligier-Renault of Thierry Boutsen completing the top six.

Both Mansell and Patrese were using the latest Renault RS4 engines in a race for the first time and were relieved that the new 'pump fuel' regulations, imposed controversially by FISA since Hockenheim, made little difference to the status quo at the front of the field.

At the start Patrese edged ahead into the first corner and Nigel prudently eased back, not wishing to jeopardise his title aspirations, as the McLarens of Senna and Berger came slamming round the outside of him to take second and third places. Knowing full well that the Hungarian race is a gruelling affair of almost two hours' duration, he settled back to run fourth in the opening sprint ahead of the warring Benettons of Schumacher and Brundle.

Riccardo was clearly out to make this the first victory of his 1992 season. With 11 laps completed he was 19.5 seconds ahead and expanded this advantage to 24 seconds by lap 25. Then, on lap 38, five laps after Mansell had overtaken Berger, the Italian was caught out by the slippery surface and spun. By the time he recovered he was

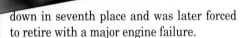

MR WORLD CHAMPION (INSET). NIGEL IS FETED BY HIS FANS AS THE GREAT MOMENT OF HIS CAREER FINALLY ARRIVES

down in seventh place and was later forced to retire with a major engine failure.

Now Mansell was a comfortable second, apparently set fair for the championship. But there was one more twist of fate which threatened to postpone his final claim on the title. At the 65-lap mark he felt his Williams suddenly sliding wildly. It was a slow puncture, raising the dreaded spectre of that Adelaide failure six years before.

Ironically, following the malfunction of the cockpit puncture warning light which had forced him into the pits at Hockenheim for an unnecessary tyre change, the instrument had been taped over for the Hungarian race. But Mansell recognised the symptoms and headed for the pit lane at the end of lap 61.

With 16 laps to go, he emerged in seventh place and began his charge to the World Championship. Senna, meanwhile, had inherited enough of a cushion to make a precautionary tyre change with ten laps to go, curing his concern that a bad vibration might damage one of his McLaren's delicate electrical components.

Mansell's comeback was electrifying. By lap 68 he was up to fourth, then he vaulted past both Brundle and Berger to retake second place. Now he could concentrate on bringing the car home and, on the 77th lap, finally pointed Williams number five out of the last corner and accelerated under the chequered flag to achieve his lifetime's ambition.

As he joined Senna and Berger on the victory rostrum, the years of effort fell away from his face and he punched the air with delight. Immediately afterwards the enormity of his achievement overcame him and he choked back tears of joy.

For Nigel Mansell, at long, long last, it was Mission Accomplished.

MANSELL **SEVENTYNINE**

THE WINNING WILLIAMS

FOR HIS ONSLAUGHT ON THE CHAMPI- ONSHIP, MANSELL HAD THE BEST CAR OF ALL THANKS TO WILLIAMS, RENAULT, HEAD AND NEWEY

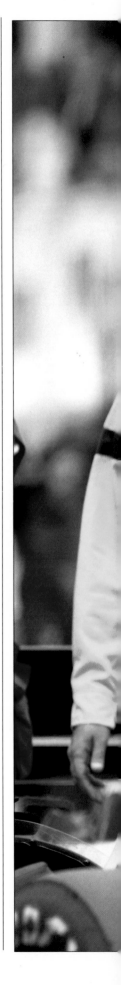

Nigel Mansell's decision to reverse his retirement plans at the end of 1990 was due largely to the efforts of Williams Grand Prix Engineering's Commercial Director, Sheridan Thynne, who helped convince him that the team from Didcot could raise the standard of its game to the point of challenging for the World Championship.

The Williams FW14B was central to this metamorphosis. Since losing its supply of Honda engines in 1987, Williams had been through three lacklustre seasons with only intermittent success. However, although 1988 had been a stop-gap year, using Judd V8 engines, they had managed to rekindle a relationship with a major motor manufacturer for the following year when they began using the 67-degree Renault V10. As a result, they were occasional winners in 1989 and 1990, although seldom looking like serious front-runners capable of challenging the omnipotent McLaren-Hondas.

Williams technical director, Patrick Head, is ruthlessly self-critical when he analyses the disappointments of 1990 and the relatively poor form of the Williams FW13.

'These things are always reasonably complex,' he reflects. 'I think we did an adequate, but not special job during our first year with the Renault V10 in 1989, finishing third in the championship. It was an acceptable first year.

'Bearing in mind that what we would then operate in 1990 was based on the design work we did in 1989, I think the following year was pretty poor. I was aware that it was pretty poor – and poor because of inadequate design input. I mean, the FW13B car was just not very good.'

Did he blame himself for this? 'Oh I think largely, yes,' he fires back, 'because ultimately I am responsible for all of that. Looking back, I don't think we were well balanced on the engineering side. The problem now in this business is that one person can't be in charge of all the different aspects required to achieve success.'

One key area where Head felt the team was

**DYNAMIC DUO!
THE WINNING
DRIVER WITH HIS
WINNING CAR,
THE WILLIAMS-
RENAULT FW14B**

lacking was in aerodynamic development. The summer of 1990 saw ex-Leyton House team technical director Adrian Newey signed up to concentrate on the aerodynamic concept of the projected Williams FW14 – and the investment paid off splendidly.

Up to that point, Williams had been investigating the possibilities of the currently fashionable F1 'raised nose' in its wind tunnel tests, but its potential had not been maximised due to the fact they had not developed an ideal front wing configuration to match it.

Newey had already experimented with such a raised nose configuration on his Leyton House CG891 and CG901 designs and quickly made a lot of progress on this front. Head decided that they should use the concept on the new FW14 for the 1991 season and it was hoped that this new car would be a vehicle offering long-term development potential and a degree of technical stability.

The new car was based round a carbon-fibre composite monocoque, the outside surface of which was licked by the airstream, dispensing with separate removable bodywork, in much the same way as every Williams F1 machine since the Williams-Honda FW10 back in 1985.

Pushrod suspension in conjunction with inboard-mounted spring/dampers was used all round, the tiny coil-springs at the front mounted beneath a tiny, removable cover immediately ahead of the cockpit.

In finalising the front wing design, Adrian Newey had demonstrated considerable technical ingenuity. The front wing end plates were curled neatly round to incorporate 'rubbing strips' between the front axle centreline and the rear edge of the front tyre. This con-

GOODYEAR'S RUBBER WAS AN ESSENTIAL PART OF THE EQUATION. RIGHT: REMOVING THE TYRE WARMER BLANKETS. BELOW: CHECKING THE TREAD TEMPERATURES

figuration got the best out of the new regulations which required the front wing side skirts to be raised 25 cm above the underside of the monocoque's flat-floor area. It was a key factor in giving the FW14 an early handling advantage which was unfortunately dissipated in the first few races of 1991 when the car retired with gearbox failure.

The Williams-made electro-hydraulic actuation system which operated the six-speed transverse gearbox was a more refined interpretation of the system used by Ferrari since 1980. It had been tested for about 1000 km installed in an FW13B chassis, and had many more hours on the test rig as well. On the basis of this development work Patrick Head decided to incorporate it into the team's definitive 1991 chassis design.

The other key element in Mansell's 1992 World Championship-winning package was the 67-degree Renault V10 engine. At the start of the 1991 season, Renault had introduced what was, to all intents and purposes, a brand new version of the engine. It incorporated revised bore and stroke, new cylinder heads, a revised camshaft drive to reduce top-end vibration, plus a new induction and lubrication system.

This engine was dubbed the RS3 and was subjected to an intensive development programme throughout the year, a programme which was obviously carried out in close collaboration with Elf, the fuel company which has worked hard to make its own contribution to the team's overall winning package.

In its RS3B guise, with revised combustion chambers, it was developing well in excess of 750 bhp at 14,500 rpm by the time it was used on a handful of occasions towards the end of the year. This was followed by the RS3C and, finally, the RS4 – all inching forward in terms of combining better fuel efficiency with enhanced power outputs – through to the middle of 1992.

'At just under the 140 kg mark, the weight of the RS4 is the same as the RS3C and it is slightly more compact,' explained Renault Sport's development manager, Jean-Jacques His.

'Performance-wise, there is a significant difference between the two engines and, for a given level of fuel consumption, the RS4 is more powerful and produces more torque.'

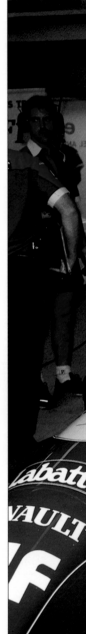

In fact, the RS4 was rather more than a derivation of its immediate predecessor. Although conforming to the same configuration as the RS3 range, it had a new block, further revised bore and stroke dimensions, a new cylinder head and a new crankshaft. 'Apart from the electronics and gudgeon pins, all the principal component parts of the Renault RS4 are totally different,' His continues.

It was perhaps symbolically appropriate that, having assessed the RS4 during practice and qualifying for many races, it was first used in anger at Budapest, the race in which Mansell's second place clinched him the championship.

As far as chassis development is con-

MANSELL **EIGHTYTHREE**

cerned, Patrick Head envisaged a 'B' version of the FW14B for the start of 1992, following it up with a definitive new FW15 chassis some time during the course of the season. As things transpired, up until the point that Mansell clinched the World Championship, the FW14B had remained largely unchallenged in its position at the front of the field and the necessity for the FW15 had not proved overwhelmingly obvious from the touchlines.

However, just as today's F1 design process is a complex and wide-ranging business, involving a large team of technicians specialising in various differing facets which contribute to an overall competitive package, so it is the business of a team's technical director accurately to assess the strength of the competition – and anticipate correctly what rival teams might have in the pipeline.

It has to be said that Head's assessment of what was needed in 1992 proved right on the button. Having toyed with active suspension systems in 1987 and '88, he knew this was an area where a worthwhile technical benefit could be gained. Thus, for 1992, active suspension was incorporated in the Williams FW14B design, together with a traction system which controls wheelspin by momentarily cutting several of the engine's cylinders rather than by closing the throttle.

'The suspension system should be described as a rapid-response, controlled ride-height system,' explains Patrick Head. 'It is a derivative of the 1988 version. It is quite adequate to call it an active suspension system. In its purest form, you have an hydraulic strut carrying the load of one corner of the car.

'By measuring the pressure in that strut, by measuring the vertical accelerations at the wheel and the chassis, and then by controlling the servo valve in the strut, you can make that strut behave like a suspension system without any necessity for a conventional spring and damper.' In fact the FW14B system relies on small disc springs within the four hydraulic cylinders, so when the car goes over a bump the system pushes oil into the cylinders and compresses those disc springs.

The FW14B's electro-hydraulic gearchange is very similar to the system used in 1991, most of the team's efforts having been concentrated on the active suspension sys-

THE WILLIAMS FW14B SECRET WEAPON IS ACTIVE SUSPENSION (LEFT). INSET: NIGEL TALKS WITH F1 SUPREMO BERNIE ECCLESTONE

tem. Next year, predicts Patrick Head, will see a much bigger step forward on the transmission front.

'We have done a certain amount of software development whereby the system can do automatic up-changes and can, if we choose to, do automatic downchanges – that's to say, not driver-initiated,' he explains. There is also an automatic clutch function – which, up to the time of preparing this book, has not yet been used in a race – whereby the driver can simply hold the engine at maximum revs, press a button on the steering wheel and accelerate away without his foot touching the clutch pedal!

Without doubt, the Williams-Renault FW14B represents state-of-the-art Grand Prix engineering of the 1990s. It is a technical *tour de force* in which aerodynamic efficiency, computer-controlled suspension technology, a compact and efficient engine/transmission package and a high standard of operational competence have combined to produce a car which has truly proved itself fit for a World Champion.

MANSELL **EIGHTYFIVE**

THE ROLE OF THE RACING TYRE

GOODYEAR

THE CRUCIAL CONTACT PATCH
BETWEEN CAR AND TRACK SURFACE
CALLS FOR A SPECIAL KIND OF TYRE
AS MANSELL AND WILLIAMS KNOW

Up to the 1992 Hungarian Grand Prix, the Williams team could boast 59 World Championship Grand Prix victories – every one of them achieved on Goodyear tyres. The successful transfer of racing technology to high performance road tyre production has been the underlying factor in Goodyear's international racing involvement ever since the company, based in Akron, Ohio, became seriously committed to the sport's most prestigious category back in 1965.

Nigel Mansell's World Championship title in 1992 represents the latest milestone for Goodyear in a run of almost unbroken success which started when the company supplied its first purpose-made F1 racing tyres to the Brabham and Honda teams in 1965. The Japanese company almost immediately repaid that support when the late Richie Ginther sped to Goodyear's maiden Grand Prix victory in Mexico City, in the final race to be held under the 1½-litre engine regulations.

Goodyear's first World Championship was secured by Jack Brabham in 1966, the Australian thereby becoming the first driver to win the title at the wheel of a car bearing his own name, but the company only really began to dominate Grand Prix racing after forging a partnership with Jackie Stewart and the Tyrrell team in 1971 which yielded two drivers' titles in three seasons.

Thereafter, Goodyear's successes came thick and fast. By 1977 Niki Lauda had

GOODYEAR
SUPPLIES AN
AVALANCHE OF
TYRES FOR EACH
GRAND PRIX.
INSET, THE
TEAMS PROVIDE
THE RIMS ON
WHICH THEY ARE
MOUNTED

scored Akron's 100th Grand Prix victory at the wheel of a Ferrari. Its 125th was notched up by Alan Jones with a Williams-Cosworth in Canada two years later and René Arnoux's victory in the same race in 1983 took the total to 150. By 1987 Gerhard Berger's victory in Australia raised the tally to 200 wins and Ayrton Senna's McLaren-Honda success in the 1991 Brazilian Grand Prix marked a landmark 250th win for the company.

By pushing components to the outer limit of their performance, motor racing provides Goodyear with a consistently effective and demanding testing ground. If a component or material works satisfactorily in a highly stressed racing environment, it can generally be assumed that it will work under nor-

THE GOODYEAR TYRE FITTING BAY IS PROBABLY THE MOST CONSISTENT-LY CROWDED AREA THROUGHOUT THE THREE DAYS OF A GRAND PRIX WEEKEND

mal operating conditions in a road application with a significant safety margin.

For this reason experimental tread compounds and belt/carcase fibres are frequently tested in racing tyres as an integral part of their development programme. The technology thus developed makes a significant contribution to the manufacture of high performance road tyres: Jaguar's confidence in this process can be judged from the fact that Goodyear Eagle high performance tyres are fitted as original equipment on the Jaguar XJS range of road cars.

The contribution made by drivers such as Nigel Mansell and the Williams team – which is one of a handful of contracted Goodyear teams as opposed to simply being a

TYRE PRESSURES ARE ABSOLUTELY CRUCIAL ON GRAND PRIX CARS AND ARE MONITORED WITH CONSTANT PRECISION

in the future. In that respect, a challenge from a rival is anticipated in 1994. When development costs are added to the requirement to work on a new range of F1 tyres to meet the revised 15-in. maximum width regulations for 1993, the investment required will increase considerably.

Even so, Goodyear is absolutely committed to Grand Prix racing and believes implicitly in its value as a technical and marketing tool.

Goodyear's international director of racing, Leo Mehl, takes up the theme. As one of the architects of the company's F1 involvement, he endorses Gaug's views.

'We much prefer a fight in this business because the benefits that accrue from racing are split pretty well 50/50 between the advertising benefit and the technical impact. But you run the danger to an extent of losing some of those benefits in a monopoly situation. Having said that, there is no other form of promotion where we can get such an outstanding return on our investment as with Formula 1.'

Quite clearly, like few other areas of the sport, racing improves the production breed in terms of tyre technology in a quite dramatic fashion. Moreover, the link between road and racing tyres can, in some cases, be specifically identified.

Since the directional rain tread pattern was introduced into F1 at the start of the 1980s, with its subsequent commercialisation as a street tyre with the Eagle VR/ZR, there have been more signs than ever of Goodyear's technology transfer from racing to road tyres.

The development of the Eagle high performance tyres began with the Eagle NCT, followed by the NCT2. This was later supplemented by its big brother, the Eagle ZR, a race-bred high performance tyre which can be found as standard equipment on some of the world's most famous thoroughbred performance cars. The Eagle range of tyres has developed quickly and now includes the Eagle GT+4, an all-year-round performance tyre, and the Eagle GS-D, an ultra-performance high speed tyre.

The partnership between Goodyear and Williams has been highly productive and congenial. 'Frank runs one of our top testing teams,' insists Lee Gaug. 'He is co-operative,

customer – is a key element in sustaining Goodyear's unprecedented level of Grand Prix success. Goodyear's F1 racing manager, Lee Gaug, explains how the partnership works.

'We make our contract with the team and, obviously, we do not try influencing their driver selection or the way they operate. To be honest, this year we haven't tested a great deal because having to provide identical tyres to all cars places a strain on our production facilities, and makes it more difficult to change our tyre line as a result of any testing that we do. But if we've got competition from another tyre supplier, we could test for 15 or 20 days a year and more if necessary to maintain our competitive edge.'

Gaug also makes the point that Goodyear have to be ready to anticipate the possibility of rival tyre-makers coming in at some stage

MANSELL NINETY

THE WILLIAMS CREW BRUSH UP ON THEIR TYRE CHANG-ING TECHNIQUE WITH A LITTLE PRACTICE AT IMOLA, 1992

he has good drivers and good cars. We would probably never make a decision on changing tyre construction, sizes or compounds without discussion and tests with them. We never tailor our tyres to any one chassis, of course, but we rely on the input of teams like Williams to provide the data from which we can make the best possible compromise in the design of the production race tyre which is then made available to the field.'

Moreover, while superstar drivers like Nigel Mansell may not like the thought of burdening themselves with excessive testing between races, Gaug and his colleagues believe their input is absolutely essential. 'Even if we went testing with Williams and they were using Damon Hill, excellent though he is, we would not make a decision on his input. At the end of the day it would have to be Nigel or Riccardo Patrese who would give it the final seal of approval because they are ultimately quick,' he explains.

Over the last few years Williams has probably carried out 40 per cent of Goodyear's testing in F1. 'Frank has told me that he would sign a ten-year deal with Goodyear any time we liked to put the contract in front of him,' laughs Lee Gaug. 'He and his team have been totally loyal to Goodyear and never wavered in that commitment.'

MANSELL **NINETYONE**

NIGEL MANSELL
RACING RESULTS
1980-1992

A FULL RECORD OF NIGEL MANSELL'S GRAND PRIX OUTINGS FROM HIS MAIDEN RUN IN A LOTUS 81 TO HIS WORLD CHAMPIONSHIP CLINCHER

	RACE	CIRCUIT	DATE	CAR	COMMENT
			1980		
ret	AUSTRIAN GP	Österreichring	17/08/80	Lotus 81B-Cosworth	engine
ret	DUTCH GP	Zandvoort	31/08/80	Lotus 81B-Cosworth	brakes/spun off
dnq	ITALIAN GP	Imola	14/09/80	Lotus 81-Cosworth	
			1981		
ret	US GP WEST	Long Beach	15/03/81	Lotus 81-Cosworth	hit wall
11	BRAZILIAN GP	Rio	29/03/81	Lotus 81-Cosworth	
ret	ARGENTINE GP	Buenos Aires	12/04/81	Lotus 81-Cosworth	engine
3	BELGIAN GP	Zolder	17/05/81	Lotus 81-Cosworth	
ret	MONACO GP	Monte Carlo	31/05/81	Lotus 87-Cosworth	rear suspension
6	SPANISH GP	Jarama	21/06/81	Lotus 87-Cosworth	
7	FRENCH GP	Dijon	05/07/81	Lotus 87-Cosworth	
dnq	BRITISH GP	Silverstone	18/07/81	Lotus 87-Cosworth	
ret	GERMAN GP	Hockenheim	02/08/81	Lotus 87-Cosworth	fuel leak
ret	AUSTRIAN GP	Österreichring	16/08/81	Lotus 87-Cosworth	engine
ret	DUTCH GP	Zandvoort	30/08/81	Lotus 87-Cosworth	electrics
ret	ITALIAN GP	Monza	13/09/81	Lotus 87-Cosworth	handling
ret	CANADIAN GP	Montreal	27/09/81	Lotus 87-Cosworth	accident with Prost
4	CAESAR'S PALACE GP	Las Vegas	17/10/81	Lotus 87-Cosworth	
			1982		
ret	SOUTH AFRICAN GP	Kyalami	23/01/82	Lotus 87B-Cosworth	electrics
3	BRAZILIAN GP	Rio	21/03/82	Lotus 91-Cosworth	first two disqualified

7	US GP WEST	Long Beach	04/04/82	Lotus 91-Cosworth	
ret	BELGIAN GP	Zolder	09/05/82	Lotus 91-Cosworth	clutch
4	MONACO GP	Monte Carlo	23/05/82	Lotus 91-Cosworth	
ret	US GP (DETROIT)	Detroit	06/06/82	Lotus 91-Cosworth	engine
ret	CANADIAN GP	Montreal	13/06/82	Lotus 91-Cosworth	accident
ret	BRITISH GP	Brands Hatch	18/07/82	Lotus 91-Cosworth	handling
9	GERMAN GP	Hockenheim	08/08/82	Lotus 91-Cosworth	
ret	AUSTRIAN GP	Österreichring	15/08/82	Lotus 91-Cosworth	engine
8	SWISS GP	Dijon	29/08/82	Lotus 91-Cosworth	
7	ITALIAN GP	Monza	12/09/82	Lotus 91-Cosworth	
ret	CAESAR'S PALACE GP	Las Vegas	25/09/82	Lotus 91-Cosworth	accident with Baldi
			1983		
12	BRAZILIAN GP	Rio	13/03/83	Lotus 92-Cosworth	
12	US GP WEST	Long Beach	27/03/83	Lotus 92-Cosworth	
ret	FRENCH GP	Paul Ricard	17/04/83	Lotus 92-Cosworth	handling
ret	SAN MARINO GP	Imola	01/05/83	Lotus 92-Cosworth	spun off
ret	MONACO GP	Monte Carlo	15/05/83	Lotus 92-Cosworth	accident with Alboreto
ret	BELGIAN GP	Spa	22/05/83	Lotus 92-Cosworth	gearbox
6	US GP (DETROIT)	Detroit	05/06/83	Lotus 92-Cosworth	
ret	CANADIAN GP	Montreal	12/06/83	Lotus 92-Cosworth	handling/tyres
4	BRITISH GP	Silverstone	16/07/83	Lotus 94T-Renault	
ret	GERMAN GP	Hockenheim	07/08/83	Lotus 94T-Renault	engine
5	AUSTRIAN GP	Österreichring	14/08/83	Lotus 94T-Renault	
ret	DUTCH GP	Zandvoort	28/08/83	Lotus 94T-Renault	spun off
8	ITALIAN GP	Monza	11/09/83	Lotus 94T-Renault	
3	EUROPEAN GP	Brands Hatch	25/09/83	Lotus 94T-Renault	Fastest lap
nc	SOUTH AFRICAN GP	Kyalami	15/10/83	Lotus 94T-Renault	
			1984		
ret	BRAZILIAN GP	Rio	25/03/84	Lotus 95T-Renault	slid off track
ret	SOUTH AFRICAN GP	Kyalami	07/04/84	Lotus 95T-Renault	turbo inlet duct
ret	BELGIAN GP	Zolder	29/04/84	Lotus 95T-Renault	clutch
ret	SAN MARINO GP	Imola	06/05/84	Lotus 95T-Renault	brakes/accident
3	FRENCH GP	Dijon	20/05/84	Lotus 95T-Renault	
ret	MONACO GP	Monte Carlo	03/06/84	Lotus 95T-Renault	hit barrier when 1st
6	CANADIAN GP	Montreal	17/06/84	Lotus 95T-Renault	
ret	US GP (DETROIT)	Detroit	24/06/84	Lotus 95T-Renault	gearbox
6/ret	US GP (DALLAS)	Dallas	08/07/84	Lotus 95T-Renault	gearbox/Pole
ret	BRITISH GP	Brands Hatch	22/07/84	Lotus 95T-Renault	gearbox
4	GERMAN GP	Hockenheim	05/08/84	Lotus 95T-Renault	
ret	AUSTRIAN GP	Österreichring	19/08/84	Lotus 95T-Renault	engine
3	DUTCH GP	Zandvoort	26/08/84	Lotus 95T-Renault	
ret	ITALIAN GP	Monza	09/09/84	Lotus 95T-Renault	spun off
ret	EUROPEAN GP	Nürburgring	07/10/84	Lotus 95T-Renault	engine
ret	PORTUGUESE GP	Estoril	21/10/84	Lotus 95T-Renault	spun off
			1985		
ret	BRAZILIAN GP	Rio	07/04/85	Williams FW10-Honda	accident damage
5	PORTUGUESE GP	Estoril	21/04/85	Williams FW10-Honda	
5	SAN MARINO GP	Imola	05/05/85	Williams FW10-Honda	
7	MONACO GP	Monte Carlo	19/05/85	Williams FW10-Honda	
6	CANADIAN GP	Montreal	16/06/85	Williams FW10-Honda	
ret	US GP (DETROIT)	Detroit	23/06/85	Williams FW10-Honda	brakes /crashed
dns	FRENCH GP	Paul Ricard	08/07/85	Williams FW10-Honda	accident in practice
ret	BRITISH GP	Silverstone	21/07/85	Williams FW10-Honda	clutch
6	GERMAN GP	Nürburgring	04/08/85	Williams FW10-Honda	
ret	AUSTRIAN GP	Österreichring	18/08/85	Williams FW10-Honda	engine
6	DUTCH GP	Zandvoort	25/08/85	Williams FW10-Honda	
11/ret	ITALIAN GP	Monza	08/09/85	Williams FW10-Honda	engine/Fastest lap
2	BELGIAN GP	Spa	15/09/85	Williams FW10-Honda	
1	EUROPEAN GP	Brands Hatch	06/10/85	Williams FW10-Honda	
1	SOUTH AFRICAN GP	Kyalami	19/10/85	Williams FW10-Honda	Pole
ret	AUSTRALIAN GP	Adelaide	03/11/85	Williams FW10-Honda	transmission
			1986		
ret	BRAZILIAN GP	Rio	23/03/86	Williams FW11-Honda	accident with Senna
2	SPANISH GP	Jerez	13/04/86	Williams FW11-Honda	Fastest lap
ret	SAN MARINO GP	Imola	27/04/86	Williams FW11-Honda	engine
4	MONACO GP	Monte Carlo	11/05/86	Williams FW11-Honda	
1	BELGIAN GP	Spa	25/05/86	Williams FW11-Honda	
1	CANADIAN GP	Montreal	15/06/86	Williams FW11-Honda	Pole
5	US GP (DETROIT)	Detroit	22/06/86	Williams FW11-Honda	
1	FRENCH GP	Paul Ricard	06/07/86	Williams FW11-Honda	Fastest lap

1	BRITISH GP	Brands Hatch	13/07/86	Williams FW11-Honda	Fastest lap
3	GERMAN GP	Hockenheim	27/07/86	Williams FW11-Honda	
3	HUNGARIAN GP	Hungaroring	10/08/86	Williams FW11-Honda	
ret	AUSTRIAN GP	Österreichring	17/08/86	Williams FW11-Honda	driveshaft
2	ITALIAN GP	Monza	07/09/86	Williams FW11-Honda	
1	PORTUGUESE GP	Estoril	21/09/86	Williams FW11-Honda	Fastest lap
5	MEXICAN GP	Mexico City	12/10/86	Williams FW11-Honda	
ret	AUSTRALIAN GP	Adelaide	26/10/86	Williams FW11-Honda	crashed/Pole
			1987		
6	BRAZILIAN GP	Rio	12/04/87	Williams FW11B-Honda	Pole
1	SAN MARINO GP	Imola	03/05/87	Williams FW11B-Honda	
ret	BELGIAN GP	Spa	17/05/87	Williams FW11B-Honda	accident
ret	MONACO GP	Monte Carlo	31/05/87	Williams FW11B-Honda	wastegate pipe/Pole
5	US GP (DETROIT)	Detroit	21/06/87	Williams FW11B-Honda	Pole
1	FRENCH GP	Paul Ricard	06/07/87	Williams FW11B-Honda	Pole
1	BRITISH GP	Silverstone	12/07/87	Williams FW11B-Honda	Fastest lap
ret	GERMAN GP	Hockenheim	26/07/87	Williams FW11B-Honda	engine/Pole/Fastest lap
14/ret	HUNGARIAN GP	Hungaroring	09/08/87	Williams FW11B-Honda	lost wheel nut/Pole
1	AUSTRIAN GP	Österreichring	16/08/87	Williams FW11B-Honda	Fastest lap
3	ITALIAN GP	Monza	06/08/87	Williams FW11B-Honda	
ret	PORTUGUESE GP	Estoril	21/09/87	Williams FW11B-Honda	electrics
1	SPANISH GP	Jerez	27/09/87	Williams FW11B-Honda	
1	MEXICAN GP	Mexico City	18/10/87	Williams FW11B-Honda	Pole
dns	JAPANESE GP	Suzuka	01/11/87	Williams FW11B-Honda	accident in practice
			1988		
ret	BRAZILIAN GP	Rio	03/04/88	Williams FW12-Judd	overheating
ret	SAN MARINO GP	Imola	01/05/88	Williams FW12-Judd	electrics/engine
ret	MONACO GP	Monte Carlo	15/05/88	Williams FW12-Judd	accident with Alboreto
ret	MEXICAN GP	Mexico City	29/05/88	Williams FW12-Judd	engine
ret	CANADIAN GP	Montreal	12/06/88	Williams FW12-Judd	engine
ret	US GP (DETROIT)	Detroit	19/06/88	Williams FW12-Judd	electrics
ret	FRENCH GP	Paul Ricard	03/07/88	Williams FW12-Judd	suspension
2	BRITISH GP	Silverstone	10/07/88	Williams FW12-Judd	Fastest lap
ret	GERMAN GP	Hockenheim	24/07/88	Williams FW12-Judd	spun off
ret	HUNGARIAN GP	Hungaroring	07/08/88	Williams FW12-Judd	driver exhaustion
ret	PORTUGUESE GP	Estoril	25/09/88	Williams FW12-Judd	spun off
2	SPANISH GP	Jerez	02/10/88	Williams FW12-Judd	
ret	JAPANESE GP	Suzuka	30/10/88	Williams FW12-Judd	spun off
ret	AUSTRALIAN GP	Adelaide	13/11/88	Williams FW12-Judd	brakes/spun off
			1989		
1	BRAZILIAN GP	Rio	26/03/89	Ferrari 640	
ret	SAN MARINO GP	Imola	23/04/89	Ferrari 640	gearbox
ret	MONACO GP	Monte Carlo	07/05/89	Ferrari 640	gearbox
ret	MEXICAN GP	Mexico City	28/05/89	Ferrari 640	gearbox/Fastest lap
ret	US GP	Phoenix	04/06/89	Ferrari 640	gearbox
dsq	CANADIAN GP	Montreal	18/06/89	Ferrari 640	black-flagged
2	FRENCH GP	PaulRicard	09/07/89	Ferrari 640	
2	BRITISH GP	Silverstone	16/07/89	Ferrari 640	Fastest lap
3	GERMAN GP	Hockenheim	30/07/89	Ferrari 640	
1	HUNGARIAN GP	Hungaroring	13/08/89	Ferrari 640	Fastest lap
3	BELGIAN GP	Spa	27/08/89	Ferrari 640	
ret	ITALIAN GP	Monza	10/09/89	Ferrari 640	gearbox
dsq	PORTUGUESE GP	Estoril	24/09/89	Ferrari 640	black-flagged
ret	JAPANESE GP	Suzuka	22/10/89	Ferrari 640	engine
ret	AUSTRALIAN GP	Adelaide	05/11/89	Ferrari 640	spun off
			1990		
ret	US GP	Phoenix	11/03/90	Ferrari 641	clutch
4	BRAZILIAN GP	Interlagos	25/03/90	Ferrari 641	
ret	SAN MARINO GP	Imola	13/05/90	Ferrari 641	engine
ret	MONACO GP	Monte Carlo	27/05/90	Ferrari 641	electronics
3	CANADIAN GP	Montreal	10/06/90	Ferrari 641	
2	MEXICAN GP	Mexico City	24/06/90	Ferrari 641	
19/ret	FRENCH GP	Paul Ricard	08/07/90	Ferrari 641	engine/Pole/Fastest lap
ret	BRITISH GP	Silverstone	15/07/90	Ferrari 641	gears/Pole/Fastest lap
ret	GERMAN GP	Hockenheim	29/07/90	Ferrari 641	slid off
17/ret	HUNGARIAN GP	Hungaroring	12/08/90	Ferrari 641	accident with Berger
ret	BELGIAN GP	Spa	26/08/90	Ferrari 641	handling
4	ITALIAN GP	Monza	09/09/90	Ferrari 641	
1	PORTUGUESE GP	Estoril	23/09/90	Ferrari 641	Pole
2	SPANISH GP	Jerez	30/09/90	Ferrari 641	

ret	JAPANESE GP	Suzuka	21/10/90	Ferrari 641	driveshaft
2	AUSTRALIAN GP	Adelaide	04/11/90	Ferrari 641	Fastest lap
		1991			
ret	US GP	Phoenix	10/03/91	Williams FW14-Renault	gearbox
ret	BRAZILIAN GP	Interlagos	24/03/91	Williams FW14-Renault	gearbox/Fastest lap
ret	SAN MARINO GP	Imola	28/04/91	Williams FW14-Renault	collision with Brundle
2	MONACO GP	Monte Carlo	12/05/91	Williams FW14-Renault	
6/ret	CANADIAN GP	Montreal	02/06/91	Williams FW14-Renault	engine/Fastest lap
2	MEXICAN GP	Mexico City	16/06/91	Williams FW14-Renault	Fastest lap
1	FRENCH GP	Magny-Cours	07/07/91	Williams FW14-Renault	Fastest lap
1	BRITISH GP	Silverstone	14/07/91	Williams FW14-Renault	Pole/Fastest lap
1	GERMAN GP	Hockenheim	28/07/91	Williams FW14-Renault	Pole
2	HUNGARIAN GP	Hungaroring	11/08/91	Williams FW14-Renault	
ret	BELGIAN GP	Spa	25/08/91	Williams FW14-Renault	voltage regulator
1	ITALIAN GP	Monza	08/09/91	Williams FW14-Renault	
dsq	PORTUGUESE GP	Estoril	22/09/91	Williams FW14-Renault	Fastest lap
1	SPANISH GP	Catalunya	29/09/91	Williams FW14-Renault	
ret	JAPANESE GP	Suzuka	20/10/91	Williams FW14-Renault	spun off
2	AUSTRALIAN GP	Adelaide	03/11/91	Williams FW14-Renault	race stopped/spun off
		1992			
1	SOUTH AFRICAN GP	Kyalami	01/03/92	Williams FW14B-Renault	Pole/Fastest lap
1	MEXICAN GP	Mexico City	22/03/92	Williams FW14B-Renault	Pole
1	BRAZILIAN GP	Interlagos	05/04/92	Williams FW14B-Renault	Pole
1	SPANISH GP	Catalunya	03/05/92	Williams FW14B-Renault	Pole/Fastest lap
1	SAN MARINO GP	Imola	17/05/92	Williams FW14B-Renault	Pole
2	MONACO GP	Monte Carlo	31/05/92	Williams FW14B-Renault	Pole/Fastest lap
ret	CANADIAN GP	Montreal	14/06/92	Williams FW14B-Renault	slid off
1	FRENCH GP	Magny-Cours	05/07/92	Williams FW14B-Renault	Pole/Fastest lap
1	BRITISH GP	Silverstone	12/07/92	Williams FW14B-Renault	Pole/Fastest lap
1	GERMAN GP	Hockenheim	26/07/92	Williams FW14B-Renault	Pole
2	HUNGARIAN GP	Hungaroring	16/08/92	Williams FW14B-Renault	Fastest lap

SUMMARY

Grand Prix starts: 176; Grand Prix wins: 29; Pole positions: 26; Fastest laps: 28

**Nigel Mansell
made himself a
firm favourite
of Ferrari fans
during his two
seasons with
the famous
Italian team,
but will always
be associated
with Williams
number five**